BEYOND MERELY BEING

A Guide to Being Happy

by

Ronald R. Himebaugh

authorHOUSE™

1663 LIBERTY DRIVE, SUITE 200
BLOOMINGTON, INDIANA 47403
(800) 839-8640
WWW.AUTHORHOUSE.COM

© 2004 Ronald R. Himebaugh
All Rights Reserved.

First published by AuthorHouse 10/08/04

ISBN: 1-4184-9405-4 (sc)

Library of Congress Control Number: 2004096443

Printed in the United States of America
Bloomington, Indiana

This book is printed on acid-free paper.

Foreword

I pulled up to a lovely home located somewhere out between the suburbs and rural farm country. It was a community of beautiful, large homes on wooded lots ranging from two to twenty acres each.

The house I stopped at in particular was set back from the road and nestled in a stand of mature trees that had been there since before my time. I wanted to take a minute and reminisce about some times I had spent inside that house. You see, I knew the people that lived there a few years ago. I had been to the gatherings, cookouts and holiday parties they had given over the years, and the memories were good ones.

The man that lived there was a self-employed consultant, and he had a wife and kids. When he left for work each day he wore a white shirt, tie and jacket. He seemed like a nice enough guy, and most would judge him to be in his late forties to early fifties.

I remember at one of the first gatherings I attended there was a mix of neighbors, friends and relatives. It was interesting to observe everyone as they discussed the usual topics (state of economy, world morality, music, etc.). I distinctly remember hearing someone remark as to how fortunate we all are to be living a life so many others would cherish. "Look at this house and this family," one person said. "I doubt he has ever experienced the hardships that so many others have. I doubt he realizes how life is such a struggle to the majority of people in the world."

I remember it made me think of a song I had always wanted to write called "Troubles Come to Everybody Sometime."

The idea for the song had come about from experiences in my own life. It seemed to me that true troubling times come upon everyone from time to time. It seems like we all live in peaks (of fortunes) and valleys (of despair) throughout our lives. Even the rich and famous, the beautiful and healthy, and the young and gifted are not exempt from such troubles. Think about it – death of a loved one – bankruptcy – divorce – lifelong illnesses - lifelong responsibilities to truly disabled children – lost true love – mental illness - depression – on and on…

The guy that used to own the home I am talking about is a good example. To look at him one would say he is lucky. He looks young for his age, and he has an easy smile. But his past may have surprised a few. He came from a middle class, blue-collar family. In elementary school he was a porky little kid that struggled to pass from grade to grade up until about the seventh grade.

As I understand it, he improved his grades in high school to mostly C's and a few B's. It was tough on him because both his older brother and younger sister received straight A's (or nearly so). Although he took the College Prep course schedule in high school, you wouldn't say he was necessarily college material. In fact, you would be right, but he attended anyway, and struggled in his first two years; graduating with a "two point something" grade point average. Of course, back then we all had a little more motivation to attend college because the alternative was the draft into the Service for a tour of duty in Vietnam.

Ah, Vietnam – yes, that is a lousy word for many people my age. He wasn't so lucky when he graduated from college because within a few months he was drafted into the army, and was on his way to Vietnam. He told me he had several opportunities to follow a course of leadership and become an officer; however, that would just add several more years onto his requirement to the Army, and more exposure to time in Vietnam. As he told me once, "This is about risk-management."

I never heard him comment too much to people about his service time, but since I had a similar plight, he did tell me a few things. He was in the infantry and carried the machine gun. He had made the rank of sergeant. He had been a gunner on caravan gun trucks, humped the central highland jungles, and was sergeant of the guard along the docks of Quin Yon Bay. Acting in behalf of the Commanding Officer, he had to identify bodies and write letters to the parents of those young men that didn't make it. He said he had never experienced fear and loneliness such as at that time in his life – not before, and not since.

After more than a year in Vietnam he returned home. It was 1971, and they say he seemed somehow different.

Soon after returning he went back to school and obtained his Masters degree; graduating with a high grade point average. He was successful at his job and progressed along a career path. He came to a crossroads in his life, as he tells it, and made a decision to start up his own business. Someone said he went through some grueling years of working late into the night, and traveling much of the time. He wasn't rich, but he was happy and not worried.

Then came the wave of troubles. Through no fault of his own he was forced into bankruptcy. The bank he used was bought out, the Loan Officer was indicted for a credit card scam, and records of several business loan transactions (for his business and others) were lost or destroyed. The burden of business continuation could not endure the demands by the bank. It was a terrible time for him and his family. He wasn't used to facing failure, and he worked hard to avoid it, but in the end he lost everything, his house, his car, his income. He did find a way back. It was a hard process, and he lost some self-assurance and esteem. It was hard to look at his friends and some of his relatives because they were not aware of all the details, and bankruptcy to many means incompetence. The losses and personal shame took a toll on his marriage and that, too, failed (after 17 years).

Several years later he was back on his way starting another related business, and through diligence and good service to his clients was able to not only enjoy what he was doing, but also bring in a decent income. He remarried, and things were good.

Is that it? No, not quite. Several years passed (he was in his mid forties by then), and he developed diabetes. One thing he had learned was that "troubles come to everybody sometime," and that with perseverance and determination he could overcome all obstacles – he already had, several times! He researched diabetes and became well versed on the latest medications and treatment methodologies. He was determined not to let this disease adversely affect his life. He had good success at controlling the diabetes, but out of nowhere came another adversity. His natural heart pacemaker stopped, and he had to have an artificial pacemaker put in. He found out both the diabetes and related heart problems were almost certainly related to exposure to the chemical toxin, Agent Orange; which he had encountered in Vietnam.

So, as I sit here reminiscing about the good times I had in that house of his, I have to laugh just a little when someone looks at him and thinks he is lucky. But you know what? He thinks he is lucky! You see, everything is relative, and troubles come to everybody sometime!

This book will help you realize how lucky you are, and how you can be happy by pursuing your own personal endeavor in life. I hope it helps you determine more precisely what makes you truly happy in terms of a life endeavor. You will learn that many people confuse an endeavor or purpose with a "need" or perhaps a "goal." Most psychologists agree that there are certain needs we all have to obtain before we can carry on with pursuing a purpose. For instance, we all require food, security, love and esteem as needs to our human behavioral makeup.

As an example, Joe might think that his life purpose is to play the piano because he is good at it, it comes easy for him and he really enjoys performing. One question he might ask himself is, "How do I like practicing?" His answer might be that practicing is not necessarily fun, but it is required in order to become good at playing the piano; like any other job or endeavor. You might think this makes sense, but you will find that there are pianists that even love to practice. Joe might actually be satisfying a need. Self-esteem from others is an important need that people misplace. Perhaps Joe's love of performing is satisfying that need.

Typically, someone that is following their life purpose doesn't care about what others think, but they do it because they find great joy in it. That doesn't mean Joe can't enjoy playing the piano, and making it a big part of his life. It is quite possible that some other part of music is his purpose. He might discover, with some self-introspection, that it was arranging or composing music that really interests him. He just focused on satisfying a "need" instead of a "purpose."

What I hope to do in this book is to show you a way to determine what your purpose in life is, and provide a method to pursue that purpose. The method is well-tested in business and industry, and now will assist you in making your way on this journey called life.

This may not sound like something profoundly new, but what I hope makes the difference for you, as it did for me, is the integration of some knowledge of human behavior, and some techniques to assist in motivation, determination and desire.

So how does all this lead to happiness? True happiness comes from pursuing an endeavor with desire. Happiness that comes from material purchases (such as cars, boats, etc.) and from circumstances (such vacations, parties, alcohol etc.) is a temporary happiness that overrides your true state of being.

True happiness gives energy to your life, and makes you a successful and fulfilled person. It makes those around you happier.

Table of Contents

Chapter 1 - Introduction

What is the secret to life? Curly said it all in the movie "City Slickers." He said, pointing his index finger into the air, "The secret of life is this." Of course, Billy Crystal said, "What, your finger?" Curly said, "No, one thing, just one thing! If you stick to that everything else don't mean nothin'." The next question is, "what is the one thing?"

To put it in the words of Arnold, "What choo talkin' 'bout, Willis?" To be very general, I think whatever the secret is that we would all concur that for it truly to be the "secret of life" it must have the result of making each one of us happy. In other words, "what is the secret to a happy life?" Now, let's work backwards from that.

What makes people happy? You've probably asked yourself that question a few times in your life. Again, I think most of us would agree that happiness means different things to different people. This would imply that the "one thing" is not the "same thing" for all of us, but rather something that may be different for each of us. See the logic in working backwards? Is this inductive reasoning or deductive reasoning? Who cares, Ron? Let's keep following this line of thought.

There are many things that make us happy like love, money, power, recognition, etc. Even appreciating a beautiful day, an exquisite sunset, your family around you or just everything you are blessed with can be defined as happiness. And I don't disagree that these things do make people happy, or maybe - make people *"feel"* happy.

1

What's the difference?

Well, I believe (as do others) that happiness is deeper than what was just described. The sunsets, and the beautiful days are temporary feelings that override whether or not we are happy inside. Perhaps many things provide these temporary feelings of happiness; you know, like buying a new car, buying a boat, putting in a pool, etc. Hey, maybe drinking alcohol and feeling uninhibited is another way to "feel" happy. How about drugs?

Do you see what I'm saying? I'm not so sure that the majority of people don't live their lives by using "things" or "conditions" to make themselves happy. We won't worry about those people; they've convinced themselves they're happy so why should I meddle in their affairs? Besides, I'm sure they're not reading this book. If you're reading this book you're probably more interested in what "really" makes people happy (either that or you're one of my friends or relatives and feel obligated to read the book).

The fact of the matter is that there are things that are "important to us" like needs, goals and interests, and then there is that deep down "life purpose." These things are many times confused. Just because something is important to us doesn't mean it is part of a life purpose to happiness.

Important Note

The word "purpose" is used a lot now days, especially in reference to a "reason for living." It has almost a magical, mystical or spiritual connotation. That's not exactly what I mean by "purpose" in this book. I'm talking more about something that we each are truly interested in pursuing, but don't - either because of all the other life activities around us or because we don't feel it is possible to attain (due to time or money).

Let's see, if you are a medical doctor you may feel that health and fitness is what makes people happy. You know, sound mind, sound body? So you would write a self-help book on the proper eating and exercise habits, and motivate us to do this to become happy. Personally, I'm big on this idea. I think health and fitness are very important.

☑ **Don't take good health for granted.**[1]

If you are a financial wizard, then you may say that the way to happiness is through money management. Why? Because money is the root of all evil! Ok, maybe I'm being a little dramatic, but, it does seem, sometimes, like people just aren't very happy without enough of it. Once again, I think there may be something to this. I mean, look at all the people buying lottery tickets, and trying to get rich. There are definitely many money management books in the bookstores. You can't argue that money sure does allow one to afford the luxuries of life. Wait a minute! What are the luxuries of life? Aren't they the "things" (materials) that bring us temporary happiness?

☑ **Discipline yourself to save money.**
It is essential to success.[1]

If you are an engineer or management specialist you would probably say that happiness is found through the proper management of your life. You would tell everyone that goals need to be set, and that methods of reaching the goals need to be defined, and your life needs to be organized so that you won't get confused about where you are going. Structure and planning are the keys to happiness. Well, of course I agree with this. I am involved in business management as part of my real job (as opposed to writing books).

☑ Strive for excellence, not perfection.[1]

If you are a dreamer or philosopher then happiness is embodied in the search for truth about mankind and the universe. Discovering knowledge and contemplating our surroundings is what makes us happy. They would say that we all have a drive within us to seek the truth about everything. I'm not opposed to a little of this. I believe thinking about what makes things tick is important. It leads to questions and then knowledge.

☑ Remain open, flexible, curious.
Be open to new ideas.[1]

If you are a romantic then true love is what makes us happy. The need to give and receive love from someone special is overpowering. The attraction and emotions of love are so powerful. People in love just seem to be happy constantly. Even a bad day seems wonderful to them. The idea of a soul mate and someone that feels like you are the most wonderful person in the world is very fulfilling, especially when the feelings are mutual. So, you would write a book about how to keep the love active in your life, and how to communicate with your mate to overcome misunderstandings, jealousy, etc. There are certainly many books related to this subject. This "happiness from love" I definitely believe has much merit.

☑ Never underestimate
the power of love.[1]

If you are a psychiatrist or psychologist then you have studied this idea of happiness to the limit. Human nature (behavior) is what you study. You have studied motivation in animals and people, and have come up with numerous theories. The need for sex and/or love has been a big topic of motivation by many experts including Sigmund Freud, Masters and Johnson, and Alfred Kinsley; to name a few.

Probably the most famous and currently accepted theory on human behavior is Maslow's Hierarchy of Needs. Maslow determined that man has a deep desire to seek "self-actualization." What is that? Basically it is the desire to "*be all that you can be*," and I'm not talking about joining the Army. Self-actualization is different for each of us. For some it may be fairly recognizable because they were born with a very gifted talent like playing a musical instrument or painting. For most of us, however, it may not be that obvious. We may have to really do some thinking.

The problem in attaining self-actualization is that we are sidetracked by other needs that have to be satisfied first - you know like food, water, shelter, safety, love and self-esteem. See, Maslow says that there are these different levels of needs that all of us must satisfy in a specific order before we reach the final level of self-actualization. If you don't know what I'm talking about don't worry about it. We will go into it in a little more detail later. Not too much detail though – I don't want to make this some sort of textbook.

What about religion? Religion actually aligns pretty well with what my aforementioned professionals say. For example, religion spells out a purpose. It provides a "reason" in life. It provides the "how" and the "structure" to get there, and it provides for peace of mind. It releases some people from worrying about things that they shouldn't be worrying about. This is a spiritual purpose to life, and not meant to be in conflict or competition with the purpose I am referring to.

I want to make sure that everyone understands that this book does not suggest that the "life purpose" discussed here is, in some way, related to a spiritual purpose. Or, that it is, in some way, advocated as a replacement for a spiritual purpose. The purpose I am talking about is something that we each are best at pursuing. It could involve a talent or it could involve the internal desire to "do" something with all earnest and interest (overwhelming desire).

I took Catechism, was confirmed in the Lutheran church, and took several courses in New Testament thought and philosophy in college. This makes me no expert in religion (and am certainly not qualified to write on the subject), but my exposure to religion has indicated that most Christian denominations believe God gave each of us talents and skills to be used here on earth to the best of our abilities. Recognizing and using these talents or gifts is what I am referring to as purposes. There is no reason we cannot have both a spiritual purpose and a purpose for our means here on earth. Perhaps prioritization of purposes is in conflict with some people. Spiritual purpose is a whole other topic that will not be discussed in this book.

So now you're thinking, "well which of these self-help theories (i.e. health, management, love, etc.) really leads to happiness?" My answer is that all of these things are involved in the pursuit of happiness to some extent. You see, all of these methods work to some extent because when we focus our mind on something, then we make it happen. The problem is that we can't seem to stay focused long enough to see things through to completion. Most of these self-help ideas are working because they assist us in focusing on some plan, at least for a while.

What is the typical attention span of a human being – about 5 to 15 minutes isn't it? In reading they say that the attention span of viewing an overhead slide is 8 to 10 seconds or about 26 words. Here's a little humor from the Internet:

Broken Newz–Research shows the attention span of the average reader

Sun Valley, Idaho – A report released last Thursday from the ISA (International Satire Association) detailed the viewing habits of the vast collection of Satire readers. The report shows how 24% of readers seldom read beyond the title relying on its descriptive presence for humor. 46% of those studied only peruse the first three or four lines, while 69% blah blah blah blah blah blah blah blah blah blah blah blah blah blah blah blah blah blah blah blah blah blah blah blah.

Anyway, the saying "**Out of sight, out of mind**" is so true. Just think about it in your everyday life. Your mind can only work on a number of issues at a time; so, the rest of your thoughts take up space hanging around. Not only that, most of us are raised to always complete the task we have started. We must "eat everything on our plate before we are excused". We must "finish cleaning the bathroom first." "Don't do anything halfway." This further reinforces our training to focus just on a few tasks at a time until they are complete.

Do you know what's funny about this? When I took my first supervisory management course the book said that a good manager is one who can have many uncompleted jobs going on at once. A good manager never completes one task before another is started. I don't mean to imply that it was wrong for my parents to train me to complete a job before going on to the next because "completion" does assist most of us in a feeling of accomplishment. By the same token, it seems like most of us have been raised to be worker bees instead of management bees.

I'll insert one more observation here. Most of us are raised to be good concerned people, and we put others' needs before our own; especially our spouse's, our parent's, our family's, and our friends.'

So we humans have a short attention span (can only manage to focus on a relatively few issues at a time), and we put others before ourselves. When do we focus on our own health and fitness (body maintenance)? Well, not as often as the maintenance on our car, our house, or our children. When do we focus on our personal happiness needs? Do you see what I'm saying? We tend to neglect our personal needs.

Everything seems to be turned around. On the one hand experts tell us that we must be happy within ourselves, and then that will make others around us happy. That is to say that when we are happy we find time to live happily and make others happy. On the other hand, we are told to put others before ourselves, and to work on only a few things at once, and to feel guilty if we do things for ourselves (self-centeredness). Am I being redundant here? Yes, because this is an important point.

Well, there it is! We just figured out what the "One Thing" is – it is the one purpose each of us is supposed to do. Well darn it; Curly was just saying what everyone else has been saying. I was hoping there was more to it. It all comes down to finding what we are interested in and pursuing it. Well, that's it. You know everything you need to know. How'd you like the book?

Just Kidding! Ok, so maybe there is nothing new or profound about what was just discussed. Maybe we already knew all this but, if so, why aren't we just the happiest little cowboys and cowgirls in the world (no pun intended Curley)?

Yep, just because we know what to do, doesn't mean we will do it. It's like dieting. We all know that dieting is as simple as a mass balance equation; that is, the amount of food we eat is directly related to the amount of weight we gain or lose. So, all we have to do is eat less to lose weight. And so all we have to do to be happy is pursue the one thing we know is right for us to do.

Ok, I made my point. Once you really know what you want to be when you grow up, then the hard part begins – making it happen. That's what this book is going to do – help you understand why it is hard to do, and then give you a plan on how to make it easier to do. It is only hard to do initially. Once you get going it will be the main thing you will want to do because it is what makes you happy.

First, we need to understand which things are preventing us from pursuing our happiness. Some, I'm sure you already know, and others will be new to you. I call this "awareness." We need awareness of how we operate and how others around us operate. This includes things like our self-image, expectations, mind clutter, and much more.

Then, we need some tools. That is, we need techniques to keep that "purpose" in the forefront of our minds.

9

Specifically, we need to constantly motivate ourselves, measure how we are doing, and follow certain written guidelines (plans). Why? Because –

"Out of sight, out of mind."

In this book I will provide you with exactly how to discover and define a purpose, how to plan for your success, and how to acquire the resources to implement your purpose.

I have really been talking a lot about this "purpose in life" thing, and you're probably getting tired of it, but it is imperative that you understand that the purpose I am talking about is not the same as accomplishing "goals" or satisfying "needs" in your life.

Life Purpose (Life Endeavor)

First and foremost your purpose has to be a "life" purpose. You have to discover what it is you really want to be or do. This is maybe related to self-actualization? Most professionals agree that we humans have an innate desire to, as I said before, "be all that we can be." The problem is most of the time we don't know what the "be" is. The "be" is something we will want to pursue until we die. Wow! That sounds pretty dramatic!

The thing is, a life purpose is on-going (a program). It has no end (like a project). We can set our goals to have a great family or beautiful home. Or we can set our goals to accomplish certain career objectives or to obtain a certain level in business. Or we can set our goals to reach a certain salary or to solve specific problems. These goals all have a beginning and an end. When we accomplish the goal, that's it – we are done. Then what? Set a new goal? Change direction? Sure we can do that, and most of us do it all the time, but if we can find the one thing that really drives us, then we will be happiest, and we will get up each day ready to get to it.

Have you ever been in love? If you have, you know that feeling. Gifted artists feel it. The nerdy scientist that doesn't care about what he wears and how he looks has it. He just wants to keep doing research on whatever it is that drives him. There's a saying that goes like this:

If this is empty (heart)

Then this doesn't Matter (brain)

Being somewhat of a problem solver (as part of my job) I developed the opinion that we could get wherever we wanted to go in life if we just used our brains. We just needed to think it out, and logic would prevail - sort of along the lines of Mr. Spock (Star Trek). But you know what? It's the heart that controls what we do. I am talking about the heart's desires. It overrides the brain every time.

It is much stronger. Look at love. How many times has your brain said, "No, no, no," but your heart said, "Yes, yes, yes!" Which wins? How about when you are feeling down or depressed? Your brain says, "Look how fortunate you are compared to others. Look at your opportunities. Just stop being depressed!" It doesn't work does it? Your heart is broken or wounded or just without a purpose.

So, if we can get the correct purpose to reside in the heart, then we are on our way!

Attention! – Very Important Notice

This word "purpose" is used so much in self-help books, and it has many pre-conceived meanings to many of us. Other commonly used words such as goal, mission, meaning, plan, direction, etc. are also overused and can infer conflicting meanings. For that reason, I will be using the word "<u>endeavor</u>" throughout this book to mean the "purpose" I am talking about.

Determination

It is very difficult for most of us to keep going when pursuing a life endeavor because there are so many barriers that arise daily. We just get bogged down with other issues we have to deal with, and we start giving up on our life endeavor. Then, we feel like we have failed at being self-disciplined enough to control our own lives to do what we really want to do. We have to - NOT GIVE UP! Almost everyone that is successful has failed over and over again, but they just didn't give up. Abraham Lincoln had eleven (11) major failures in his personal and political life. How many times have you heard that someone is an overnight success? Take acting. We see a new actor and we think, "I wonder how he or she made it to the top so quickly." Then we are watching an old Twilight Zone episode on TV and there the person is – trying to make it back then. There's another saying that goes like this:

☑ Remember that overnight success
takes about fifteen years.[1]

So, everyday you must get up and say, "THIS IS THE FIRST DAY OF THE REST OF MY LIFE!" Forget failure and just keep trying over and over! After a while it will work. The right ENDEAVOR and self DETERMINATION are the two factors that will make the biggest difference in your ability to follow your endeavor. In this book I will give you some excellent tools to determine what your life endeavor is, and how to implement a life plan to pursue that endeavor. You must then apply determination (or focus), but awareness will help you.

Chapter 2 - Why This Book?

So what's the difference between this self-help book and others that talk about "setting" and "obtaining" goals? Well, in this book a lot of time is concerned with determining a "true-life" endeavor. Too many times we think we are making plans around a true-life endeavor, but later it becomes apparent that what we really had was a need or a goal. A true-life endeavor is one that is ongoing throughout life, and it is what we personally want to do.

Take Jim and Bob, they are both good pianists and everyone loves to hear them play. Both are in their early twenties, and have been playing since they were six. Jim knows he is good and loves playing the piano. It is such an enjoyable, creative release. However, Jim bought my book (good choice Jim) because he wanted to confirm that he was on the right track. Bob, on the other hand, did not buy this book (Bob's loss). He has had no such wonderings about his life.

It seemed obvious to Jim that he was supposed to be a piano player; so, he assumed that would be his life endeavor. His interest in this book was to determine the best, managed way to reach his endeavor. In reading the book he had to do some real self-introspection. He had to ask himself some questions he had not really asked before. One of the things he had to think about was how well did he like to practice, and how determined was he to be the best piano player in the world?

When he was honest with himself he concluded that practicing was like a job that was required to make him play better; so, he didn't necessarily get great joy from practicing. As far as becoming the best piano player in the world, he knew he wasn't that good. After all, let's be realistic – he wanted to be as good as his talent and perseverance would allow him. No use in having expectations that couldn't be reached, right? Did he ever daydream about being the best? No, not really.

Bob, on the other hand was different. Upon asking his mom and dad if it was difficult to get him to practice when he was young, they said, "Get him to practice? Heck, we couldn't get him to stop. We would have to tell him to quit so we could go to sleep at night." Why didn't Bob want to read my book? Is he crazy? This is a great book! Well, maybe he doesn't need to read it. He has no questions in his mind of what he wants to do; he's doing it! The fact that Jim bought this book could be the first sign that maybe he is wrong about thinking that playing the piano is his life endeavor.

So, there is more to determining your life desires than some people think. You will have to think about this in a different way, and I will explain later.

Another thing, we want to make sure we are not developing endeavors out of guilt or obligation. In the back of our minds we may be saying to ourselves, "Once the kids are grown, or once my husband gets a better job, or once I won't need to work anymore, or once I retire, or once Mom and Dad no longer need my assistance, or once I have enough money, or once I'm on my own… then, I'm going to do what I want to do!"

We are trained to put others before ourselves. This is not a bad trait. It is actually a very loving and caring trait - one to be proud of. However, I personally think you can provide for the needs of others, but still satisfy your own needs. By doing this you will be happier, and you will feel better about life. Much of it has to do with managing your life a little differently; that is, controlling your life. When you have control of your life, then you know where you are going.

As mentioned earlier, we do best when our minds are organized and uncluttered. It's bad enough that we fret and wonder about the day-to-day things going on around us, let alone the future things we can't control. How do we unclutter our minds? We organize our minds by eliminating the unimportant things and prioritizing the rest.

Just hang on now! I know you're thinking, "Oh no, not another book on structuring your life." It is not going to be a book about difficult or complex life changes. In fact, it is easy.

In industry they have spent a lot of time and effort on creating ways to focus on the important aspects of the company without spending time and money on tasks, processes and routines that add nothing to the success and/or profit of the company. They also spent a lot of time making these efforts easy to implement and easy to perform. Why? - Because in the work place there is not only a diversity of people, but a constant turnover of employees. To be effective, any system has to be easy to learn and easy to retrain.

In general, all of these methods involve some common methodologies. Have you ever heard of "time management?" How about "management by objectives?" Have you ever heard of "ISO 9000 or ISO 14000?" These are all methods to manage processes, tasks and/or people in business and industry. They all deal with defining goals, measuring progress and anticipating alternatives. The ISO standards are the most recent methods used. ISO stands for International Standards Organization, and they define exactly how a company will manage things like quality or environmental aspects.

These ISO methods are programs, not projects. The ISO programs are centered around "continual improvement." Why? - Because if one is forced to continuously look at the process it will always be a priority. In other words, it will always be "in sight" and not "out of mind." Projects end and then they are forgotten as the mind and attention goes to another, different project.

In this book we will apply a simplified version of these ISO management techniques to your everyday life. You will set personal endeavors, and will learn how to measure how you are doing at all times. You will "build in" options or alternatives so you will always be in control of where you are going. You will end up doing more with your life, and freeing your mind of worrying about those unimportant items (dissolving the clutter). Most importantly, it will be "on-going" and not "out of mind."

One thing you will learn in this book is to never limit your dreams. When people finally decide to do the thing they really enjoy, then they seem to find ways to make it happen. They find ways to save or acquire money, and ways to get information.

> ☑ Never give up on what you really want
> to do. The person with big dreams is more
> powerful than one with all the facts.[1]

This book will give you some excellent ideas on how to obtain the resources you need. When you are doing something you truly enjoy, then success comes next. Just like a baseball player focuses only on the current game (not any succeeding games), we must focus on what we want to do first, then later we can focus on the "how." What happens when a football wide receiver is thinking about where he's going to run while he is in the process of catching the football? He must first focus on catching it.

I have also included example scenarios of three different people with different lifestyles that we will follow as they each <u>determine</u> and <u>implement</u> their life endeavors.

This idea of "focusing" is essential, and it will help you unclutter your mind. It's a way of life. It is your life, and you are more fortunate than so many, now you need to make it a happy one. If you are thinking that this sounds like too much work, think again. Some people spend their entire lives jumping from diet to diet because they want to lose weight quickly. If they would just make a commitment to life changes in eating habits the results would occur. It may take longer to lose the weight, maybe a year, but that's still much shorter then the lifetime they are spending on it now. It is time for you to take control! This is your only human life. You can keep "wishing" and "hoping" and making feeble attempts at happiness, or you can get to it and make a better "life plan."

Get Busy Living or Get Busy Dying

— Shaw Shank Redemption

Chapter 3 - Awareness

Being aware of how you act and react to your environment and those around you; as well as how others act and react is extremely important in living a happy life. Our expectations of everything are based on this awareness, and expectations are everything in life. Misplaced expectations can lead to frustration, depression and even failure. Of all the topics in this book, this may be the most important because if we cannot control and adjust our expectations in life it is unlikely that we will be successful or happy.

This is really where knowledge of human behavior and body physiology helps us to make good decisions and to adjust our expectations. The specific areas I would like to take a look at include:

- Mind Clutter
- Appreciating What We Have
- General Human Behavior
- Human Motivation
- Self-centeredness
- Expectations in Others and Ourselves
- Being Right
- Improving Your Chances

Mind Clutter

Did you ever notice that when you awake in the morning that things seem clearer, that you think better, and that life seems better? Well, certainly resting the mind and body has a big effect on this, but I also believe our minds are released from most of the thoughts that were bouncing around from the day before. Perhaps dreaming is a way that many of these thoughts are released through use in nonsensical images and stories. That's another topic for another book.

What if these thoughts keep accumulating throughout the day? You know, as we get involved with work-associated projects, friends, family matters, etc. our minds become filled with these activities. Some may have to do with scheduling, such as work meetings, business lunches, family visits, homework enforcement, school events, dinner arrangements, house cleaning, etc. Other activities may be related to emotional or psychological activities, such as: listening to the problems of friends and family members; dealing with the children's school problems; trying to resolve spousal relationship issues; etc. These personal stress-type activities probably take up more mind space than we realize because they can be linked to emotional reactions such as guilt, sorrow and depression. Remember, many of us can only deal with a portion of these issues at a time, while the remaining thoughts just hang around cluttering the mind.

I'm not a psychologist, so perhaps this is not exactly a certifiable analysis of our minds, but evidence does point to what I'll call "mind clutter." Maybe these other diversionary things that make us happy simply override the mind clutter for a while. For example, when one falls in love, that very strong emotion just seems to drown everything else out. The person almost can't seem to see anything wrong in life. Life is wonderful, and there is no clutter, or at least the clutter seems to dissolve. Similarly, I believe religion can dissolve clutter by way of exacting guidelines to the way we should live. This assumes that much of the mind clutter is rooted in making decisions about how to act and react to our environment. Even people with a "mission" in life are able to resolve their mind to only that which they are interested in. Meditation is used extensively throughout the world as a way to clear the mind, and make thinking efficient. It starts with focusing the mind on just one thing, like a specific word. Perhaps, if we focus on an "endeavor" in life we will less likely allow the clutter to creep in.

What I would like to do is to propose that when you have a life endeavor, and have developed a means by which to reach that endeavor that your mind will be clearer, and you will be happier. I am not proposing this as a substitute for spiritual peace, but rather something that may even enhance spiritual beliefs. We are all individuals, and what works for one may not be as effective for another; however, I believe that we should always keep our minds open to new ideas.

☑ Commit yourself
to constant improvement[1]

We live in an age of computers and technology. As part of their job many people sit at desks, talk on phones, write memos and shuffle paper. It has become more and more of a "service" oriented industry. Not so long ago, we were in the industrial age of mainly manufacturing where people performed physical tasks. They lifted pieces onto the assembly line, or packed and unpacked supplies. When they went home for the day they felt physically "spent," and there was no thinking about uncompleted tasks or papers yet to shuffle or pending meetings to prepare for.

Today, when many people go home from work they not only have incomplete tasks, presentations, calls and meetings bouncing around in their heads, but they must deal with the activities of home life. This presumable lack of remedial physical work actually makes us feel incomplete; not even close to being "spent." We have all this junk bouncing around in our heads, and yet at the end of the day we can't think of much we have accomplished.

If you're a carpenter there's no problem feeling accomplished. You built something, and its progress or completion is obvious. The creative process was measured and/or completed. There was something we used to say back when I was working for the local government, shuffling papers, - "I'll need to polish my shoes when I get home tonight so I will feel like I've accomplished something." Many people have had to resort to making check lists of tasks completed at work so that they can actually view what they have accomplished at the end of the day. This helps the mind feel a sense of completion, and the "pending" tasks can be released from the mind.

It's not just that many jobs have changed, but that our personal lives have become more complicated. Even those of us working in a manufacturing environment come home to a myriad of activities. For example, kids today have so many organized sports that it keeps parents hopping, just driving them around. Back when I was a kid there were no organized football, baseball, softball, or traveling basketball teams for kids under high school age. Heck, we hadn't even heard of soccer. Couple this with the fact that in most families today both parents work, and you have the proverbial "rat race."

So we get up early in the morning so everyone has an opportunity to shower. Then, there's making and eating breakfast; next, checking the children's homework to make sure it is completed; and then everyone is off to work or school. We work, then fight the five o'clock traffic; get home and either make supper or buy it. Next, we get the kids to do some of their homework, and then it's off to a track meet. We return home about nine o'clock, and get the kids to finish their homework. Then, there are a couple of arguments about picking things up around the house and what to wear the next day, etc. Finally, we turn the TV on and fall asleep. Then, all of a sudden we're forty-five years old, and we wonder, "What happened to my life?"

Ok, I think you are getting the picture about how I think mind clutter is important (or perhaps more accurately, unimportant). Control is what we lack. That is, we lack the ability to control our minds by sorting out what is important to worry about and what isn't. Just like we have to control our eating habits, our emotions, our spending, and our vices, we have to control our thought processes. This sounds complicated, but it doesn't have to be. Once you determine what you need, or rather want, to concentrate on, then the clutter will start to disappear.

☑ Learn to recognize the
inconsequential, then ignore it[1]

Appreciating What We Have

When people get older they start to see a pattern to life. It becomes clear that it consists of ups and downs. Of course, if you're an optimist you will see and remember mostly the "ups." Concerning the hard times, they are not restricted to just a certain age group, ethnic/race or socioeconomic group. They come upon everyone; whether it's the death of a loved one, love gone wrong, financial catastrophe, personal health issues, family health issues, mental illness, etc. The list can go on and on.

Like many people, when I get down about life I try to remind myself of how there are so many others that have it worse. I remind myself of when I was in the service and in Vietnam, and the conditions I encountered. I remind myself of third world countries, and how I am so fortunate to live in the United States. When I see someone young with a terminal illness it really brings it home to me. When I see a man and woman that have a child with a serious mental and/or physical disability, and know they will have to virtually spend their life assisting that child, it really makes me appreciate my situation.

When I got home from Vietnam I had changed. It really bothered me to see people bickering and arguing about petty things. I so appreciated food, shelter and clothing that I almost couldn't tolerate people around me. You could say I had been bumped to the lowest level on Maslow's Hierarchy of Needs. [*Remember, if you don't know what I'm talking about we will be discussing it later.*] You might say my mind was less cluttered because I had an appreciation for the basics, and how my lifestyle compared to others less fortunate. Anyway, it wasn't the fault of the people around me. They lived the same "sheltered life" I did prior to being drafted into the service. Of course, within a year or two I was pretty much back to my old self of "taking things for granted." I have to admit, though, I do use memories to keep me humbled. In fact, I still feel it would be very useful if every American could go live in a third world country for several months, just to be reminded of how lucky we are. Maybe do this every five years. Obviously, there's not much chance of that happening.

In my thirties and forties I lived like many Americans. I had a wife and two boys. We had a small ranch house, and I concentrated on moving along my career path. There were times when one of my sons would come home whining that Jimmy down the street had a better bike, or more video games (Commodore or Atari back in those days). Two or three times I would say, "Ok, let's go get an ice cream cone, what do you say?" Of course, they were for it.

We got the ice cream and then I would drive down to the very poor side of town; sort of unknowingly. The houses were old, worn down and built right next to each other. They had no air conditioning and the people were sitting out on the steps trying to keep cool. The yards were worn down, and the toys were beat up.

Pretty soon one of my boys would say, "Where are we? Are we lost? This looks like a bad area." "Oh," I said, "This is where the kids would love to have your bicycle. And they would love to see your video game – they don't have any here." It worked a couple of times. When we got home I didn't hear a peep out of them.

We all need to be appreciative of what we have, but it is very difficult to remind ourselves with the daily mind clutter. Here's an idea. Look for examples of people that can inspire you. They may be actual people you know or documentaries on famous people or fictional stories.

I remember when I went to see the movie Seabiscuit. It's a story about a real racehorse that was around during the Great Depression. Seabiscuit was too small to be considered a real potential winning racehorse, the jockey was too big to be a jockey, the trainer was too old and unconventional to be a trainer, and the owner was too new at owning race horses to know what was right. Each of these characters had a personal story of tragedy, but together they succeeded where no one would have believed they could. You might say that someone forgot to tell them that they couldn't succeed under their conditions. It is a great story with a great ending; and it's true.

Regardless of political persuasion one has to admit that Ronald Reagan was the epitome of the American dream. Read his biography sometime. He came from a low income family and his father was an alcoholic, and though well intentioned, was a shoe salesman who changed jobs constantly. In fact, the family never owned a home and lived at 37 different residences; most of them while Ron was under the age of fifteen. His mother was a strong spiritual woman that made sure Ron attended church and was active in it. What's more, Ron developed much of his speaking experience giving talks and readings in the church. Subsequently, he was a man that possessed conviction, integrity and honesty.

With a scholarship for needy students and a job to pay for his meals Ron attended Eureka College; a small religiously affiliated institution. After college he got a job at a radio station as a sports announcer, and then later was able to get a contract with Warner Brothers for a B movie actor. This was quite an accomplishment during the depression. He was called to active duty in 1942, but could not serve due to poor eyesight. Instead, he was transferred to the Army Air Corps film unit where he made over 400 training films.

Naturally, most people know he became President of the Screen Actors Guild for six terms, then later Governor of the largest State in the country (California) for two terms, and finally the President of the United States for two terms.

Arnold Schwarzenegger is another inspirational figure in current times. He came to the USA as a young man of little means. I saw a recent biography of his life on the Biography cable channel. He always wanted to come to America, and once he did he has never forgotten to appreciate this country. He has worked very hard in everything he has done, and has remained a man with his feet planted firmly on the ground. Like so many immigrants that come to the U.S. he has so appreciated the "opportunity" America provides compared to the rest of the world.

We all could take a lesson from this. In fact, when you are feeling like your life is unsuccessful or unsatisfying think like you are an immigrant. Think how you would feel if you came over here and someone gave you a house like yours, a car like yours, and a job like yours. It would be a miracle to you. We take these miracles for granted.

Another movie that demonstrates what I'm talking about is "One Magic Christmas" (sort of a modern day version of "It's a Wonderful Life"). The family in the movie is experiencing bad times during the Christmas season. The husband loses his job and they have to sell their house. The wife loses hope and sees only the desperation they are in. The husband is more optimistic, and has a plan. A Christmas Angel helps the wife to see how much she has to be grateful for compared to what "could have been," and it makes one think hard about just what is important in life.

There are lots of these types of movies. Two of my all time favorite movies include "Hoosiers" and "The Natural." Both are about people that overcome obstacles in life and succeed. They have happy endings that make you feel good about life. You want to cheer!

Read some biographies of people such as Teddy Roosevelt or J.C. Penney and inspire yourself.

Personally, I have been fortunate to know a real life inspiration. His name is Mark Humphrey and he was an employee with a client company that I have had the pleasure of working with for fifteen years. When I first met Mark he was always pleasant, personable and friendly. He was very approachable, if you know what I mean. He was probably in his thirties when we met. Over the next few years he was diagnosed with Multiple Sclerosis (MS). He began to walk slower, then after a year or so needed a cane to assist in walking. That gave way to a wheelchair, and then a motorized cart. He had a pickup truck that would load and unload his cart and then he would drive the cart into his work place.

All during this time Mark was the most positive person I have ever known. He never mentioned his problem and always derived pleasure in talking to others. He always had a smile on his face. Over the years the company found a place where he could work with his disability. About a year ago Mark could no longer make it to work. He would still stop by occasionally to say hi, and see how everyone was doing. Mark has a life of dwindling health, and he knows what to expect in terms of life span; yet, he has made the very most of it he can.

Mark has provided so much incentive and inspiration to me over the years, and he doesn't even know it. When I start feeling this old body getting stiff from age, and I feel my feet getting sore from diabetes I think to myself, "You big wimp!" Here's to you Mark!

☑ Smile a lot. It costs nothing
and is beyond price.[1]

So, maybe it would be a good idea to write down these people and events that can inspire you to move forward and appreciate what you have. Buy some such movies, and watch them occasionally to get yourself re-motivated and feeling thankful for what you have and the opportunities afforded you.

☑ Accept pain and disappointment
as part of life.[1]

☑ Don't expect life to be fair.[1]

☑ Live your life as an exclamation,
not an explanation.[1]

☑ Count your blessings.[1]

General Human Behavior

Before going much further we need to consider a little bit about how we, as humans, operate. If you understand some about human behavior you will spend less time trying to figure others out, and this will be less to clutter up your mind. I am not a psychologist, psychiatrist, or sociologist; so, I won't pretend to be an expert. I just want to touch on a few areas and theories that may be "thought provoking." The truth of the matter is that not all scientists and professionals agree on any one theory concerning human behavior.

If you start totally believing in one theory or concept, then you will limit your ability to find happiness. You must always keep an open mind, and remember that human behavior is a very complex subject. We, as humans, may make some good observations, but do we actually have all the tools and methods to really arrive at universally accepted conclusions? In life you must always try and see the "big picture," and the big picture here is the "generalizations" about human behavior that we can be aware of. Try not to get involved in specifics.

☑ **Don't major in minor things.**[1]

Most of us can determine what is right, what is logical and what is not. It is within each of us, but most of us are quick to accept what someone else tells us first. How many times have you been driving somewhere that you have been before, but perhaps not recently, and someone riding with you says, "Turn left here." What do you do? You turn left even though you know in your own mind that it is the wrong turn. Why don't we trust our own judgment? Call it intuition or, like Obie One would advise, "Let the force be with you."

One thing I have observed is that just about the time some expert defines how and why people act, someone challenges the theory by acting differently. I mean, how many times have we read about people doing something, or overcoming something that was deemed "impossible?" It almost seems like some people like to defy the odds. More appropriately, perhaps someone forgot to tell them they couldn't do what they had already achieved. The mind is a very powerful force. Fortunately, and unfortunately, it can empower us to accomplish just about anything; good or bad. In any event, I believe it is important to understand some about "accepted" human nature.

Studies in Human Nature

There have been numerous scholars that have studied human behavior and motivation either directly or indirectly. Two of the more famous such people were B.F. Skinner and Sigmund Freud. Skinner experimented extensively with the motivation of animal behavior (i.e. white rats and pigeons), and how they reacted when subjected to various situations and conditional environments. He believed the results of some such studies could be correlated to human behavior. Other scientists and psychologists have been critical of such a leap in supposition because animals are thought to possess only basic needs/drives such as food, water, propagation, etc. Other higher needs (e.g. self-esteem and love), which are prevalent in humans, make reactions, motivation and decisions to situations by humans much more complex.

Of course, Freud had his thoughts on human behavior, and many of his fundamental theories are still in acceptance

31

today. His widespread familiarity still provides study for many psychology students. Who hasn't heard of the "id", the "Freudian slip" and the "Oedipal complex?" Though much of his scientific work and many of his observations and theories have since been debunked by modern psychologists,([10]) Freud singly initiated a new, exciting, dynamic and often threatening theory of the mind and of the world. Most recognized has been his theories on how sex plays a major part in the behavior and motivation of humans.

If you are interested in these classical scientists and their impact on the study of human behavior, I recommend some additional reading. For the purposes of this book, it is not required that you know or understand these works. However, the more you know about people and human nature, the more you will be able to get along in society. Therefore, I will continue to discuss, in brevity, a few additional subjects having to do with human behavior and motivation.

Studies Concerning the Differences in the Sexes

As I mentioned, Freud had much to say about sex and the differences between sexes as motivation to human behavior. Many other people have studied and theorized the differences between sexes in an effort to better understand humans. Sex, love, lust, attraction and desire are all such powerful issues in our lives that to have at least some basic understanding is very helpful in living with other people.

Some of the more popular works dealing in sexual behavior and/or the differences in the sexes include, Masters & Johnson, Alfred Kinsley and Shere Hite. There have also been a slew of books written about this subject. Again it is helpful, if not at least interesting, to read such information.

It is fairly accepted that there is definitely a difference in the way men and women think and behave (duh!).

Most people agree that men are innately "hunters/warriors" and women are the "nest builders." In other words, men do enjoy the more macho and risky things in life and women desire safety, security and family. These statements are wide generalizations, of course, but I think a great many people believe there is some genetic link to these "male" and "female" characteristics. It cannot hurt to be aware of such differences, even if you aren't convinced that they are genetically linked. It can only help you to communicate and live more contently.

As an example, it has been said that women are the great communicators. They are a more social being than men. Women like to discuss issues and interface with others more than men. Men are considered to be more oriented towards "problem solving." As a result, when a man and woman get into a dispute the man typically argues towards a "solution"; whereas, the woman mainly wants to talk about the problem, and to feel the comfort in communicating feelings and concerns. This is not to say she doesn't want to solve the differences expressed, but rather that there is just as much interest in "discussing" the solution as there is in reaching the solution.

Men could improve their success in either overcoming or avoiding many drawn-out arguments if they would remember this about women. With a little understanding on how men and women think, both sexes could avoid many of the common routine arguments.

Statistics in Human Behavior & Characteristics

Well, while I'm on the subject of human behavior, why not introduce yet another area; statistical relationships. Don't worry; I'm not going to get into a detailed discussion in mathematics. I wouldn't do that; math was always my worst subject in high school and college.

The Bell Curve

The statistical relationship I am talking about is the "bell curve (or bell-shaped curve)." It is a statistical graph (for those of you not familiar with it). As you can see from the picture it is shaped like a bell. It distributes a set of data (samplings) in a way that shows which values are most normal (i.e. occur most frequently).

As an example, if a representative cross section of Americans was sampled for IQ (Intelligence Quotient), the results could then be plotted on a bell curve graph. The plotted line (curve) of the bell curve would represent all the data sampled. In very general terms, the peak (top of the bell) would represent the values that occur most frequently. In the case of IQ we would expect most of the values to be close to 100; making it the most common; or normal, if you will (i.e. 100 is the average IQ value).

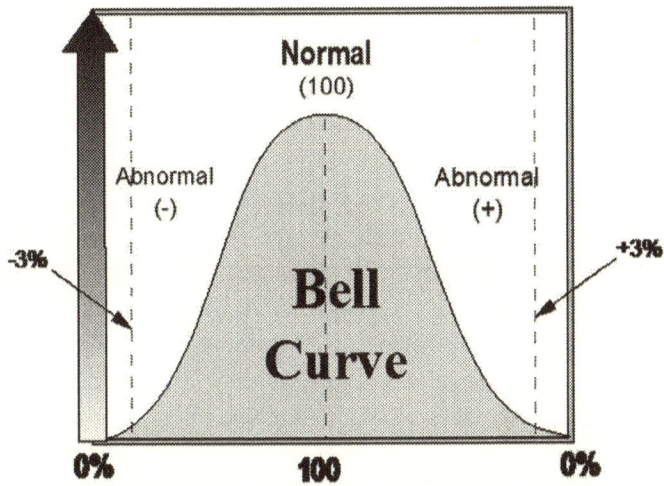

As we follow the curve downward on either side of this peak the <u>frequency</u> of values decreases until it approaches zero at each end of the curve. As we move along the curve to the left there are a fewer and fewer number of people with an IQ decreasingly less than 100. And, if we move along the curve to the right there will be the same degree of reduction in people that have an IQ increasingly greater than 100. Higher numbers to the right of the peak are indicated as positive numbers (+), and lower numbers to the left of the peak are indicated as negative (-) numbers. So, if the normal IQ is 100 (the average), then it becomes clear that as we deviate in lower and higher IQ values that there are less and less people with these extreme IQ's.

For the IQ bell curve, it has been determined that about 3% of Americans score above 130, and about 3% score below 70. The IQ scale considers people with an IQ greater than 130 (3%) to be "gifted." Similarly, those with an IQ of below 70 (3%) are considered to be retarded.

35

Applying human behavior characteristics to this bell curve can be very interesting; especially those characteristics that are linked to genetics (e.g. hair color, height, etc.). As another example, if it is assumed that some, if not all, sexual characteristics are genetically linked, then the bell curve could describe normalcy of these characteristics. There is, of course, much disagreement over such possibilities, and I am neither a proponent nor opponent of these theories. It just seems interesting to ponder the possibilities. I am sure with the strides made in DNA identification; it won't be long until more concrete evidence will be available to support theories from one side or the other.

For exemplary purposes only, let's make some assumptions that men and women have differing amounts of male and female characteristics, hormones, etc. Again, we are making this up, and I am not specifically talking about any one characteristic, but rather the assumption that there is one or more linked genes that cause a human being to be more female or more male in physical characteristics as well as desires, emotions, mental operation, etc.

Also, only for exemplary purposes, lets say a "normal" male possesses about 80% male characteristics (gene influence), and 20% female; this would be the peak of the bell curve. The number of males that possesses an even higher percentage of male characteristics (say 90% male and 10% female) would be much less (as indicated by the downward slope of the bell curve). So, further and further right on the bell curve would indicate a lower and lower percentage of these males as part of the population. Similarly, moving to the left would result in men with less and less male characteristics, and possibly more female characteristics.

One could see, using this example, that the male at the extreme right would be the epitome of the "macho" man. This man may, perhaps, be very aggressive and very attracted to women. He might be obsessed with dominance, control, hunting, propagation and so forth. At the extreme other end (left) of the curve the man may possess almost no male characteristics, and nearly all female characteristics. He may, for all intents and purposes, be a woman in man's body. The characteristics would then vary considerably throughout the curve.

As I mentioned, whether or not one believes that such genetic-linked characteristics can be described by a bell curve is debatable. There are both proponents and critics of the bell curve and its application to human characteristics, IQ, etc. Again, I have included it here because you may want to do your own investigation. Remember, the more we understand about people and what motivates them, the easier it will be to get through life.

Nature Versus Nurture

This just can't go on much longer without the acknowledgement of the great debate between which is more important in making us "who we are;" our genetic influence (Nature) or our environmental exposure (Nurture). With the recent advances in genetic information and coding the debate has heightened. I'll have to admit that I have always come down on the side of genetics; that is, I feel it plays a more significant role in all parts of whom we are. I'll also admit that I have read some very convincing information supporting the "Nurture" proponents.

With the recent identification of a total of only 30,000 genes in the human species many scholars began to believe that there just weren't enough to be able to control all the genetic influence that was thought to be happening. However, they also admitted that for each of these genes there are groups of proteins that could make the actual effectual number of genes four times the 30,000. This is something that will probably eventually be worked out with more research.

Currently, the area of greatest disagreement has to do with physical traits versus behavioral traits. It is probably agreed that many physical attributes such as hair color, eye color, etc. are controlled by a specific gene/s, but that the search for, and confirmation of, "behavioral" genes is a source of disagreement.

Of course one of the problems is that if our makeup is mainly genetically controlled, then we will subsequently have less ability to change the way we are; no matter how hard we may want to. Personally, I believe, like most others, that not all genetic influence is like the physical ones (e.g. eye color). Many are more of a condition that will be effected by our environmental influence; in other words, more of a combined or synergistic association between nature and nurture.

As an example one study concluded that certain people that had colon cancer had a certain faulty gene associated with them. However, there were others that had the same faulty gene that did not contract cancer. It was determined that the faulty gene did result in the contraction of cancer, but only when associated with certain food ingested. So, the ability to contract the cancer had both a gene and environmental influence.[5]

Also, some people believe that it is a myth that genetic differences are difficult to change, but environmental differences are easy to change. Frank Fujita gives this example:

> For example, poor eyesight is genetic, and yet there are ways to correct it, eyeglasses, contact lenses, surgery. On the other hand, a childhood with little protein makes one short, and once grown, we cannot raise the individual's height to what we might want to think of as genetic potential."[2]

Well, I'm not so sure this is the best analogy. My response would be that by wearing shoe lifts or some other surgical process there could be a way to raise his/her height. After all, aren't glasses just as much an "unnatural" solution to the eyesight problem?

If you don't think genetics plays a major part in one's makeup, then you haven't been around children much. From "day one" children exhibit specific traits of their personality and sex. Most little boys just automatically go for the trucks, and the girls go for the dolls. The little girls "mother" their little brothers, and the boys love to play with balls and other action objects.

Recently, while I was using the inside track at the YMCA, I was watching some little children play basketball on the courts below me. They were organized games and teams, and the boys and girls were very small – maybe Kindergarten age or first graders. It was fun to see their personality differences on the court. One little girl was just very aggressive, and would not be denied "driving to the basket." Of course, she "walked" and "double-dribbled" about thirty times (ha!).

Then, there was this little boy that obviously was not the athletic type. He couldn't really dribble the ball. His whole demeanor was that of a person "in control" of the entire situation. He looked like a little school superintendent, or a coach. He was attempting to bring the ball down court, and another boy was guarding him very closely. At mid court he finally stopped short, held the ball on his hip, and looked the boy guarding him right in the eye, and waved for the boy to "back off." It was very "matter of fact." The boy guarding was intimidated and immediately backed off. Heck, I think I would have too! He seemed to have such authority. It would be interesting to see what he becomes later on in life. Will he become a CEO of a large corporation, or will he be Head Security Guard at the state prison (ha).

Ok, so we know there may be some things about us that will be difficult to change, should we decide to. However, we just have to try harder in those areas. With this awareness we will confront such difficulties with the knowledge that we may have to modify our approach, but not give up.

Human Motivation

Maslow's Hierarchy of Needs

Much of what is covered here is directly taken from an article written by Dr. C. George Boeree, entitled "Abraham Maslow 1908-1970" (copyright, 1998). This would be an excellent place to look for additional information on this topic if you are interested.

> *Self-actualization* - One of the most interesting and studied theories on human behavior is the work done by Abraham Maslow. Maslow, like many other psychologists, was interested in human motivation. Through his studies and research he determined that people strive to reach their greatest potential. He called this "obtaining self-actualization." His definition of self-actualization, in simple terms, was "to be all that you can be." It is different for different people. One person might have the talent and desire to become the best pianist he/she can be. Another person might become the best chef or design engineer they can be. It was his theory that we all have the desire to strive to reach our personal potential. In many ways, that is what we are trying to do in setting our personal life endeavors in this book. That is why you will see that it is important that we must only think of ourselves in defining these endeavors.

> *Physiological Needs* - According to Maslow, however, one cannot reach self-actualization without satisfying some other basic needs that get in the way. In fact, he defined four (4) other levels of needs that need to be satisfied. This is typically depicted in the form of

a triangle. At the base of the triangle are the initial needs that should be met; they are physiological needs. These needs are mainly needs that keep us alive (i.e. food, water, oxygen, etc.). Some other needs, but not all, that fall into this physiological level include needs to be active, to sleep, to rest, to excrete, to avoid pain and to have sex. According to Maslow one must satisfy these basic needs before they can move to the next level of needs.

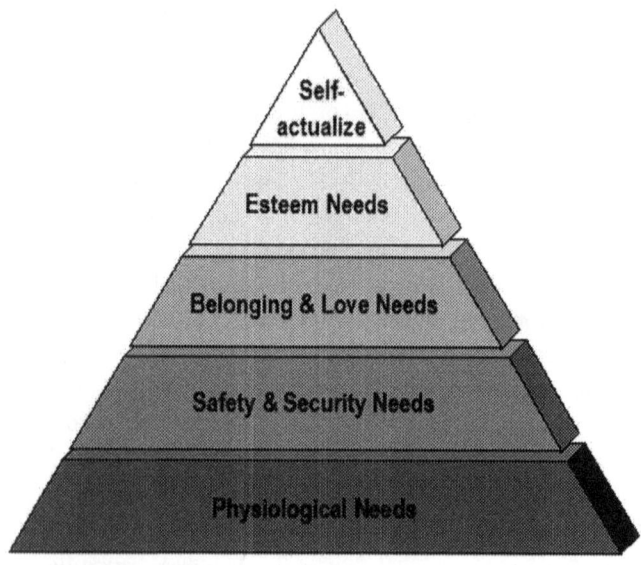

Safety and Security - The next level of needs are safety needs. Safety includes needs for stability and protection, including perhaps a need for structure, order, and limits. Looking at this in a negative way it includes some fears and anxieties. In the ordinary American Adult, this set of needs manifest themselves in the form of our urges to have a home in a safe neighborhood, a little job security and a nest egg, a good retirement plan and a bit of insurance. So, according to Maslow we all need food, water, oxygen, etc. before we even consider anything else. But once we have met these physiological needs, we next seek security. This makes sense.

Belonging and Love - The next (third) level of needs is belonging and love. For the most part once physiological and safety needs are met taking care of this third level shows up. One begins to feel the need for friends, a sweetheart, children, affection, and just relationships in general; even a sense of community.

> "He will hunger for affectionate relations with people in general, namely, for a place in his/her group, and will strive with great intensity to achieve this goal. He will want to attain such a place more than anything else in the world and may even forget that once, when he was hungry, he sneered at love.
>
> In our society the thwarting of these needs is most commonly found core in cases of maladjustment and more severe psychopathology. Love and affection, as well as their possible expression of sexuality, are generally looked upon with ambivalence and are customarily hedged about with many restrictions and inhibitions. Practically all theorists of psychopathology have stressed thwarting of the love needs as basic in the picture of maladjustment. Many clinical studies have therefore been made of this need and we know more about it perhaps than any other needs except the physiological ones.
>
> One thing that must be stressed at this point is that love is not synonymous with sex. Sex may be studied as a purely physiological

43

need.   Ordinarily, sexual behavior is multi-determined, that is to say, determined not only sexual but also other needs, chief among which are the love and affection needs. Also not to be overlooked the fact that love needs involve both giving and receiving love."[3]

On the negative side, one becomes increasingly susceptible to loneliness and social anxieties. In day-to-day life one exhibits these needs in a desire to marry, have a family, be part of a community, a member of a church, a sister in the sorority, a part of a bridge team or a golf club organization. This is also something people look for in their career.

Esteem Needs – The forth level is esteem. Esteem includes two versions. The <u>lower-level</u> has to do with the need for one or more of the following: the respect of others, the need for status, fame, glory, recognition, attention, reputation, appreciation, dignity, even dominance. This esteem is derived from others, and what they perceive us to be. The other version is referred to as the <u>higher-level</u> esteem. It has to do with what we think of ourselves (not what others think of us). It involves the need for self-respect, including such feelings as confidence, competence, achievement, mastery, independence, and freedom. Note that this is the "higher" form because, unlike the respect of others, once you have self-respect, it's harder to lose. The negative version of these needs is low self-esteem and inferiority complexes. Maslow felt that other scientists were really onto something when they proposed that these were the roots of many, if not most, of our psychological problems. In modern countries, most people have what they need in regard to physiological and safety concerns. More often than not, people have quite a bit of love and belonging, also. It's the respect that often seems so very hard to get!

All of the levels prior to "self-actualization are called deficit needs, or D-needs by Maslow. If one doesn't get enough of something, then there is a deficit, and one feels the need. On the other hand, if one gets all he/she needs, then they feel nothing at all. In other words, they cease to be motivating.

Maslow describes these levels of need in terms of homeostasis. The homeostasis principle is likened to a furnace. When it gets cold the furnace switches the heat on. Then when it gets too hot it switches it off. Maslow says your body acts similarly; that is, when it lacks a certain substance, it develops a hunger for it. When it gets enough of it then the hunger stops. Maslow sees all these needs as survival needs. Even love and esteem are needed to maintain health. He says we all have these needs built into us genetically, very similar to instincts. In fact, he calls them "instinctoid."

> "In terms of overall development, we move through these levels a bit like stages. As newborns, our focus (if not our entire set of needs) is on the physiological. Soon, we begin to recognize that we need to be safe. Soon after that, we crave attention and affection. A bit later, we look for self-esteem. Mind you, this is in the first couple of years!
>
> Under stressful conditions, or when survival is threatened, we "regress" to a lower level. When your great career falls flat, you might seek out a little attention. When your family ups and leaves you, it seems that love is again all you ever wanted. When you face chapter eleven after a long happy life, you suddenly can't think of anything but money.

These things can occur on a society-wide basis as well: When society suddenly flounders, people start clamoring for a strong leader to take over and make things right. When bombs start falling, they look for safety. When the food stops coming into stores, their needs become even more basic.

If you have significant problems along your development – a period of extreme insecurity or hunger as a child, or the loss of a family member through death or divorce, or significant neglect or abuse – you may "fixate" on that set of needs for the rest of your life.

This is Maslow's understanding of neurosis. Perhaps you went through a war as a kid. Now you have everything your heart desires – yet you still find yourself obsessing over having enough money and keeping the pantry well-stocked. Or perhaps your parents divorced when you were young. Now you have a wonderful spouse, yet you get insanely jealous or worry constantly that they are going to leave you because you are not "good enough" for them."[4].

Maslow's research into what is meant by self-actualization included picking out some people that he felt possessed the characteristics needed to achieve self-actualization. His list included such people as Abraham Lincoln, Thomas Jefferson, Mahatma Gandhi, Albert Einstein, Eleanor Roosevelt, William James, Benedict Spinoza, etc. From the study of these people he developed his definition of self-actualization. In fact, as part of this he developed a list of what he called "driving needs" or "being needs" (B-needs) of the self-actualizers, in order to make them happy:

Truth, rather than dishonesty
Goodness, rather than evil.
Beauty, not ugliness or vulgarity
Unity, wholeness, and transcendence of opposites, not arbitrariness
Aliveness, not deadness or the mechanization of life
Uniqueness, not bland uniformity
Perfection and necessity, not sloppiness, inconsistency, or accident
Completion, rather than incompleteness
Justice and order, not injustice and lawlessness
Simplicity, not unnecessary complexity
Richness, not environmental impoverishment
Effortlessness, not strain
Playfulness, not grim, humorless, drudgery
Self-sufficiency, not dependency
Meaningfulness, rather than senselessness

"At first glance, you might think that everyone obviously needs these. But think: If you're living through an economic depression or a war, or are living in a ghetto or in rural poverty, do you worry about these issues, or do you worry about getting enough to eat and a roof over your head? In fact, Maslow believes that much of what is wrong with the world comes down to the fact that very few people really are interested in these values – not because they are bad people, but because they haven't even had their basic needs taken care of!" [4]

There has been some criticism of Maslow's theory; so, what's new? That's why I'll keep reminding you that one must be careful of embracing any theory, no matter how well accepted it is. Most of the criticism comes from the scientific methodology Maslow used in his description of self-actualization; that is, the way he, himself, picked a

47

small sampling of people to study that he declared as self-actualized. And the way he then read about them, talked to them forming conclusions about what self-actualization is.

"Another criticism, a little harder to respond to, is that Maslow placed such constraints on self-actualization. First, Kurt Goldstein and Carl Rogers used the phrase to refer to what every creature does: To try to grow, to become more, to fulfill its biological destiny. Maslow limits it to something only two percent of the human species achieves...

Another point is that he asks that we pretty much take care of our lower needs before self-actualization comes to the forefront. And yet we can find many examples of people who exhibited at very least aspects of self-actualization who were far from having their lower needs taken care of. Many of our best artists and authors, for example suffered from poverty, bad upbringing, neuroses, and depression. Some could even be called psychotic! If you think about Galileo, who prayed for ideas that would sell, or Rembrandt, who could barely keep food on the table, or Toulouse Lautrec, whose body tormented him, or van Gogh, who, besides poor, wasn't quite right in the head, if you know what I mean... Weren't these people engaged in some form of self-actualization? The idea of artists and poets and philosophers (and psychologists!) being strange is so common because it has so much truth to it!

We also have the example of a number of people who were creative in some fashion even while in concentration camps. Trachtenberg, for example, developed a new way of doing arithmetic in a camp. Viktor Frankl developed his approach to therapy while in a camp. There are many more examples.

48

And there are examples of people who were creative when unknown, became successful only to stop being creative. Ernest Hemingway, if I'm not mistaken, is an example. Perhaps all these examples are exceptions, and the hierarchy of needs stands up well to the general trend. But the exceptions certainly do put some doubt into our minds."[4]

Well, perhaps that is more information than you really needed to know about Maslow's theory, but I find it very relevant to this book's objective of reaching our true life endeavors to happiness. I tend to agree with most people that Maslow was a little too structured. Most people agree that these different levels do exist, and that they are probably in the correct order. The problem is that maybe they aren't as inflexible as Maslow thought. I personally believe that there are exceptions to every rule. I think our human nature "adapts" us to living situations. What I mean is that we all have certain "expectations" about how "things should be." These expectations may be formed from our childhood experiences and environmental factors.

For example, our expectation for shelter may be a nice house in the suburbs costing $300,000. After a few years of living in a condo priced at $80,000 we adapt by lowering our expectations. This could apply to all the need levels. We tend to "settle" for something less than we expected just to get on with life. How many people marry someone because they are tired of being lonely, not because they feel that exciting feeling of true love? How about third world countries? We see people living in low levels of poverty, by U.S. standards, but yet they are happy. It is all relative. They don't know what they are missing. They have much lower expectations for their need levels than we Americans do.

Self-centeredness

From birth we are all looking for love and attention. Most of us need love, attention and recognition in order to live happily. You have seen how it is critical to your ability to accomplish your endeavors, or as Maslow puts it, "reach self-actualization."

When we see someone that demands attention we say he/she is self-centered. Now, self-centeredness has been given a bad rap. In reality, it has been responsible for making many people successful. If you have ever been to a job interview professional for advice on preparing a resume you will remember that he/she told you, "You must promote yourself because no one else will. You must put all the "good" things into your resume'." Sure it feels self-indulgent or arrogant to brag about oneself, but there are times when it needs to be done; at least in a modest way. You will need to sell yourself.

☑ Be modest. A lot was accomplished
before you were born.[1]

The problem with self-centeredness is that many people don't either recognize or acknowledge it. What I mean is that when we know everyone is self-centered (including ourselves), then we know to control/manage it properly. No one likes hearing people continually talk about themselves. Remember the George Harrison song, "I Me Mine?" So, there's a time to display or utilize self-centeredness, and a time not to. Only those that recognize it within themselves, as well as others, know how to control it.

Of course, how we are raised has some bearing on how self-centered we are. Say a child is pampered by his/her parents, and told he/she can do nothing wrong (spoiled in other words), then they may believe that they are "better," and "worth more" than others. That's it! Self-centeredness can really affect a person's image of their self worth. Some of these people may become very successful, but they may "step" on every person on the way up the ladder. They seem to be "above the law." They are many times, ruthless. We call this a distorted image of one's self worth. I should add that this, too, is a generalization. I have known two such people that were raised this way from childhood. As adults, one did exhibit self-centered characteristics, but the other did not. It just goes to show you that the influence of both genetics and the environment cannot be underestimated.

Self-centeredness, when understood, is very powerful. Many people are "seduced" and/or "used" because other people exploit self-centeredness for malice. On the other hand, it can also be an effective tool in making friends and influencing enemies. For example, if you practice "listening" to others you will be amazed at how popular you will become. Why? - Because others want to talk, and be listened to (i.e. desire attention).

Years ago I made an observation of others and myself at a party I attended. I found myself listening to others, but more importantly I found myself spending most of my listening time waiting for an opening or opportunity to speak up and put in my "two cents." Did you ever notice yourself doing that? I noticed the same thing about others, not everyone, but probably the majority. I also noticed one person in the crowd that really listened. I liked talking to him. He genuinely seemed interested in what I was saying. Others really liked him too. In fact, I remember a couple of people talking about how smart he was. Of course, it wasn't that he was so smart (who would know); it was because he satisfied that need of attention and recognition in people. Just remember, it's not just what you say, it's what you don't say, so to speak.

☑ Know when to keep quiet.[1]

☑ Know when to speak up.[1]

I took a nationally known sales course once, and part of it dealt with the use of compliments to enhance the opportunity of a sale. Compliments, of course, are a well-used method of taping into one's self-centeredness. Here are a couple of examples the sales course used to illustrate such power.

> *Example 1.* - A man is walking down the street in New York City. An obvious prostitute approaches him and says, "Hi, handsome! Need a date?" The guy knows she is a prostitute. He knows she just wants to make money, but guess what? He is still flattered. He probably thinks she overlooked a lot of other guys, but picked him because he is handsome. The compliment, sincere or not, is so powerful.

> *Example 2.* – This example is more of a compliment by showing interest. A man walks into an industrial facility to make a cold sales call (i.e. unsolicited). There is another salesman in front of him talking to the receptionist. The guy at the receptionist's desk hands her a business card and says, "Hi, my name is John Doe, and I don't have an appointment with Mr. Bigg, but I was wondering if he might give me just a couple minutes of his time?" The receptionist says, "I'm sorry sir, but Mr. Bigg's schedule is

completely full this morning, but I'll be happy to give him your card, and tell him you were here?"

Now, the second man walks up to the receptionist, and before she looks up he notices a few pictures of her family on her desk. He looks at her and with a very friendly smile says, "Good morning!" I was noticing the picture of your son. Is that a soccer shirt he has on?" "Yes", she says. "Looks like he must be twelve or thirteen years old," he says. "I have a son about that age, and I can't keep him off the soccer field. How does your son like soccer?" "Well, actually, that picture was taken two years ago. He is into basketball now," she says. "What position does he play?" the guy asks. "He plays point guard," she says, "and he has become very good. He has a game tonight, and I hope I make it home in time to get to the school to see all of it." "You sound like my wife," he says, "she works full time, rushes home for supper, and we rush to see our son play soccer. In fact, I have become the main cook at our house since I can be home earlier than her." "She is lucky," says the receptionist, "My husband is a wonderful husband and father, but he can't boil water." They both laugh, and then he says, "Well, anyway, I heard you tell the guy before me that Mr. Bigg is pretty tied up for the morning, but I would like to leave my card, if possible." "Hold on a minute," she says, "Mr. Bigg does take a couple of breaks, and he is due for one now. Let me check and see if he can see you."

The compliment of "attention" is very powerful.

For us to be happy we must satisfy our personal needs. When we are happy with ourselves, we are good to those around us, and they, in turn, feel happier. You have to like yourself first before you can like others. You've heard that many times (in fact, just a few pages back when discussing personal self-esteem). This understanding about others and ourselves is just another tool we can use in making our way through life.

This subject of self-centeredness is tricky. There is nothing wrong with needing attention – it is a predominant human trait. Human? – Hey, even animals want attention. Attention is part of being a social creature. When we are with people it is very fulfilling to exchange ideas and thoughts. It is especially fulfilling to give and receive attention with one's spouse or partner. As mentioned, the main problem stems from not knowing when enough is enough. Much of it comes down to "reading" people or circumstances.

Note

The ability of a person to read other people or circumstances is very interesting, isn't it? This is very much an "awareness" issue. These people aren't self-centered they are self-indulgent. That is to say, they are so self-absorbed in what they want to say or project that they haven't a clue as to how people are reacting to them. People give subtle feedback constantly, but the self-indulgent person hasn't a clue. These are the people that never seem to think something you are saying applies to them. As we say, "It goes right over their head."

Expectations in Others and Ourselves

Expectations are strong influences in our lives. When they are met we are happy. When they are not met we are frustrated. All the topics just discussed (i.e. mind clutter, appreciating what we have, human nature, self-centeredness and motivation) have a big effect on what we expect on a daily basis. If we can learn to buffer our expectations with a little realism we will be much happier.

We constantly place standards on people and base our expectations on those standards. The problem is that our standards don't necessarily dovetail with the standards of other people. Why should they – we are all different. This doesn't mean our personal standards are better or worse than someone else's, and it sure doesn't mean we should necessarily consider changing our standards. What we need to do is acknowledge the possibility that other people have different standards than we do, and live and let live.

> ☑ Evaluate yourself by your own
> standards, not someone else's.[1]

Think about it. How many men get all upset when their girlfriend talks to another man or even dates another man on the sly? Of course, it is all right for him to do such a thing. This "double standard" is prevalent in the world of humans. How we handle such variations in standards is to acknowledge their existence and plan for there possibility. In other words, modify our expectations.

It use to bother me that some people I knew were always late to an event such as dinner. They were such nice people, but how could they always be late, and how could they want the ridicule they received as a result from the others around them? Maybe this was attention they subconsciously wanted. Who knows, but why should I have repeatedly "expected" something different from them each time it happened?

The problem with expectations is that people confuse it with judgment. That is to say when we get frustrated because someone doesn't meet our expectations, then they feel we are judging them. Of course we are judging people all the time – it's human nature. Judging is really comparing someone against our expectations or our values or our standards. The word "profiling" has been given much bad press lately, but in reality it is simply observing someone and comparing their actions and appearance to our own standards; the standards we have developed from continual observations all our lives. You will read more on this later in this book when "first impressions" is discussed.

What about expectations within ourselves? Do we have them? You bet, and most of us have problems meeting them. That's right! We can't meet our own expectations of ourselves at times and it plays havoc with our self-worth. Many of the expectations we have of ourselves are formed by our childhood experiences, and may not be appropriate. What if you had an older brother and/or sister that did very well in athletics in high school? Then you came along, and just didn't seem to be born with those same athletic abilities. Try as you may, you just couldn't succeed as an athlete. Your expectations of yourself were quite higher than was actually possible for you to perform. This can be very bad on one's self-esteem.

When I was a kid I was fat (we'll say husky). Heck, when I was an infant they had to feed me twice as often as other babies, and they put little crocheted mittens on my hands and tied them back to keep them out of my mouth – I tried to eat my hands. My Mom and Dad, older brother and younger sister were not fat, nor had been. At school I had to hang around with the other fat kids because kids have a way of brutally categorizing other kids around them. Fortunately, I was such a happy-go-lucky kid I hardly noticed most of the time.

I was different from my brother and sister in another way. In elementary and high school they got excellent grades. In elementary school I did very poorly, and was a C and B student in high school. In high school chemistry class I got a D. The teacher was unusual for high school in that he had a PHD in chemistry (more educated than most high school teachers). He had sort of an arrogant, condescending way about him. One day we were doing what he called recitation. That was where each student had to read a question aloud at the end of the chemistry textbook chapter, and then answer it. It was very nerve-racking because we would each be trying to determine which question we would have to answer by which row was answering and in which order. When it got to me I read the question, but said I didn't know the answer. The teacher just stared at me for a few seconds and then shaking his head back and forth said, "Boy, you sure aren't like your brother, are you?"

Are you crying yet?

Obviously, I had no problems with expectations of myself – there were none. No, just kidding. Actually, my parents probably had lower expectations for me, and it made it easier for me with less pressure. When it came to college my parents were very interested in my older brother going, but really left it up to me whether or not I wanted to go. Am

I losing credibility as an author? It probably seems like I'm pretty much a regular schmuck.

Well, ok, concerning my weight I grew a couple inches between the eighth and ninth grade. I actually never was fat the rest of my life; however, I have had to more or less fight to keep the weight off. I became active in sports, and still lift weights, and take three and four mile walks almost daily. In college I was actually too skinny for a while.

Regarding my academic experience, I went to college and got a degree in Biology. One of the criteria that I had set for myself when deliberating over what my major was going to be was that it involve as little chemistry as possible. This was tough because I was very interested in science. The high school chemistry teacher had verified (at least in my mind) that I could not do well in chemistry.

After I got out of college I was drafted into the Army and did my tour of duty in the infantry in Vietnam. When I returned home I got my old job back as a laboratory assistant in the county water analysis laboratory. I loved the work, and soon realized that what I really needed was a degree in Chemistry. Using the veterans' benefits I went back to school and got a Masters Degree in Chemistry. Not only that, I was fortunate enough to have a great college graduate student advisor, and part of my thesis was eventually accepted as a standard method used around the world in the analysis of water. The university newspaper, as well as the local papers, had a big article on me and my accomplishments with a big photo. The first thing I really wanted to do (but didn't) was to take it to my high school chemistry teacher and say, "Now who's better in chemistry, me or my brother?"

Isn't that funny how impressionable we are when we are young. I never thought what my chemistry teacher said to me ever really mattered to me, but I have remembered it all these years. It kept me fearful of chemistry in my undergraduate studies. When it comes right down to deciding I was interested in chemistry, it no longer mattered, and I succeeded. Somehow I became better skilled at problem solving and since have made a living at it. I was definitely a late bloomer in life.

What does all this personal stuff have to do with the topic of expectations? Nothing really – it's my book and I can write whatever I want to! Just a little humor – actually my experiences demonstrate that expectations change constantly throughout one's life, and we should always be ready to adjust them if we want to be happy.

Being Right

The whole subject on expectations and the subsequent comparison of standards between others and ourselves can lead to big problems. People, by nature, hate to be wrong, especially about their personal convictions. This is why it is prudent not to discuss religion or politics with just anyone. People's opinions on these topics are rarely changed via discussion. About the only thing that seems to come from discussions by two or more people with contrasting views is loss of respect or confidence in each other.

This "being right" and not "being wrong" concern typically makes a reversal with age, education and experience. When we are young, say in high school, kids laugh at other kids that make mistakes or are wrong. It is all part of supporting their attempts to compartmentalize or classify their peers into specific groups- you know – the "Preps," the "Jocks," the "Nerds," the "Hoods," etc. At that age we are so sensitive to being accepted into some group.

Even as young adults we tend to over-value the need to be at a certain level and place in society.

☑ Forget the Jones.[1]

Young people in the workplace many times jump to conclusions, decisions or solutions quickly. They get frustrated at how slow things get done, and at how the "old geezers" at work don't seem to be doing the job properly or quick enough.

Somewhere during our younger ages we think we are just right all the time. We are judging others by our standards. With experience and education we start to learn that maybe things aren't quite as "black and white" as we thought. We begin to see the differences in lifestyles and cultures in our world, and we start to recognize that our views and convictions, perhaps, are based on fundamentals or "passed along views" from those people in our realm of life. Some of us start to "think for ourselves." Hurray! We start to want to look at all sides and then form our own opinions.

So, most of the time we have spent the first half of our lives trying to convince people to "see things our way," – you know, "show how we are right." We do this to build credibility so people will say, "That guy is smart. He is right, and I have a lot of respect for him." NOT! What they're probably thinking is, "That guy thinks he knows everything. He drives me nuts, and doesn't try to see anything my way – what a "know-it-all!"

If you're a teacher or have taken courses in how to train people you will recall that one of the first things you were taught is that you can't fool the students by trying to fake your way to answering questions. People know better. They can tell when you don't know what you're talking about. The proper thing to say is, "I don't know the answer, but I'll find out and let you know at the next class." People love to identify with other people. If the teacher doesn't know something, then they "gain" credibility because they are just like them – "human" (no one knows everything). They are honest, and people like that.

☑ **Admit your mistakes.**[1]

When people see a fight, and one guy brutally beats up on the other guy, who do the people support? – the underdog – every time. When you see two people that have been successful in business, politics or life, and one came from wealth and the other made it the hard way by hard work – which do we have the most respect and admiration for? People still like to be around, or can understand, people that are like themselves; that is, human (i.e. make mistakes, be embarrassed, look foolish, etc.).

The point to all this is that people get wiser and they make a flip-flop in "being right" vs. "being wrong." They realize that it's not the guy that is right all the time that they like, but rather the guy that is human and honest with them. Even if you feel there is no way you are wrong on some disagreement, is it worth pushing the point? Always think about what is important in life. Is it more important to be right on a specific point and possibly lose a friend – or is it more important to "drop it" for the good of the friendship?

☑ Be prepared to lose once in a while.[1]

There have been a few times in my life where I would have bet my life that I was right. I just knew I was. It was concerning an area that I had expertise in, and was extremely confident in. Guess what? Later I learned I was wrong. I could hardly believe it! I felt very embarrassed – especially that I had been such a "know it all."

Now, maybe the few times were just a few out of hundreds of other times I had been right (oh yeah, Ron), but it made me realize it is never, ever worth it to be so "bull-headed." I know now that even when I am positive I am right, that I could be wrong.

62

Related to the need of we humans to always "be right" is the need to tell others what to do; or rather, to expect them to live by our standards. This could be the result of trying to acquire more self-esteem or to feel we are in control, or just to impress someone. Of course the extreme cases would be the "control freaks." What I'm really talking about are all the little instances. You know, when we feel the need to "get on our soap box" and tell people the answer to the world's problems – usually at family gatherings or parties. This is normal, but if you're aware of it you can save yourself some embarrassment.

The place where this "need to tell people what to do" is very damaging is in interpersonal involvements such as marriages or committed relationships. We almost do it unknowingly.

> *"There's a parking spot, dear." (Said almost every time, just as you're entering the parking lot).*

> *"The lights are on, dear." (Said a split second after the light chime dings, and the driver is frantically reaching for the light switch in hopes that he/she beats those words).*

> *"Why are you going this way, it's longer." (Said routinely when riding together).*

Said just a few times these types of comments are meaningless, but said over and over throughout a marriage it makes the person think their spouse doesn't think they know how to do much of anything. It's so ridiculous when you think about it. Let the person find a parking space on their own. If they don't see any after going around the parking lot twice, then go ahead and help them out. Give the person a chance to turn the car lights off. What are the odds that they will make it two feet from the car without seeing that the lights are on? Definitely give them a chance to hear the light chime several times. Hey, if you finally get to the door of the house and they still haven't noticed the lights are on – go ahead, tell them – but give them a chance to succeed or fail on their own.

What's the difference? The difference is animosity won't build up over the years from such insignificant and unknowing incidences. You know after a while people start to feel like they can't do anything right in the eyes of their spouse.

These examples may seem like examples of women demeaning men, but that is not the intent. Men do it just as much, if not more. Also, if you're a backseat driver - Stop it! Don't you realize that the person drives around daily without someone else in the car and seems to make it to work or to the store or to the school just fine? And they never have accidents either. How do they do that, and how do they find a parking space when they're by themselves? And how do they seem to be able to turn the lights off on their own?

This goes for everything. People have different ways of doing things and different priorities on which things will get done in what order. If you feel the need to constantly try and change someone to meet your standards you're only going to cause someone to feel demeaned or not trusted. This living by someone else's standards applies to married people too, you know. That's why marriages between people with "like" standards are said to be more successful than those having "different" standards.

Yes, there are definite general differences in men and women and the way they seem to want to tell each other how to do things. Let's look at men first. These are generalizations, of course. Most men work, and many deal with making decisions at the work place. They may be involved in meetings where problems are solved. So, if when the man unknowingly demeans his wife it is typically because he doesn't want to explain anything to anyone – he does that all day at work. So, if the woman acts, in any way, like she may need some guidance, then the man says, "Never mind, I'll do it myself." This makes the wife feel like he has no faith in her abilities.

Of course, there are the men that have more remedial lives, and some may not even care that they could have some responsibility in making an interpersonal relationship work better. They probably have defined the duties and responsibilities of husband and wife based on their preconceived notions or experiences at home. None of these people are reading this book – that's for sure.

For women, it is many times just the opposite. Women are the "mothering, nurturing" type. They may spend most of their days teaching the children how to do things, and correcting them and guiding them. So, when they say, "There's a parking spot," they don't mean it in a demeaning way – they are just used to helping kids and it carries over. Men don't necessarily like this treatment. They're thinking, "Do you think I'm so incompetent that I can't find an empty parking space in a parking lot?" Once again, through "awareness" we can change our actions and make life easier.

There was a friend of the family that was about my age, and she went to college and became a teacher. I always liked her – she was down-to-earth and funny. I hadn't seen her for about ten years, and she showed up at a family gathering. She had spent the previous ten years as a teacher of primary school children (1st through 3rd grade). At the gathering she would come up to people and get very close to their faces (in their space) and in a sing-songy, patronizing voice say, "Hi there? How are you? Yada, yada, yada…" It was like she was talking to a six year old. I know she didn't know that's the way she came across, but everyone else did. She had just been around little children too much.

Do yourself a favor and modify your expectations of others and of yourself. Celebrate others for who they are – not who they are not.

Improving Your Chances

I'm sure when you have determined what your life endeavor is that you will want to pursue it in all aspects. Obviously, you will want to obtain whatever materials, equipment, research, standards, etc. there is related to your endeavor. In addition to such things as these you may need to alter some of your behavior and personal habits to assist you in pursuing your endeavor.

Now, I'm not talking about changing your standards, necessarily. Although we all have to be flexible enough to be open to change. I've made it a point in this book to emphasize that we all need to judge ourselves by our own standards and not by the standards of others. And, we should not judge people by our standards either. I have never said, however, that we can't change our personal standards. We will do it all of our lives. As we learn more, become wiser and change preferences we will modify our standards.

A case in point is the fact that many, many people are politically liberal when they are young and starting out. They believe that government programs that afford them benefits over others (that have more than them) are a good idea. In fact, many feel the "wealthy" almost owe the less wealthy a share of their money. After all, they don't need all that money – it's a waste to see them use it on materialistic things and expensive, nonfunctional uses when there are so many other people in need. It seems to make sense to them at the time because, after all, we are self-centered beings (I, Me, Mine).

Funny though, after these same people work hard to succeed and get to a point where they are now making a decent income they suddenly change their standards; they become conservative. After all, they worked hard for their position and salary, and they don't see why they should be required to share it with others that are just slacking along living off the government handouts (which they are now basically supplying).

So our standards change all the time. In pursuing our endeavors, we may or may not need to change our personal standards. I mean, if we have determined that music arranging and production is our life endeavor, then our outward appearance is not very important. There just isn't much public relations and exposure to the public in such a position. If, however, we have decided we want to own a restaurant, and we have been an alternative rock guitarist – then we may have some changing to consider. People that come to a restaurant want to feel like it is a very clean environment, and if the owner has dreadlocks, baggy pants dragging on the floor, then business will not be good.

Now, I laugh at times when I read or hear how some people, usually young, talk about how they don't need to conform to the conditions of any work place. I remember on one radio talk show program that the topic was about why people can't get jobs. Guys would call in and say things as, "I tried to get me one of them jobs, but they wanted me to change. Ain't nobody gonna' tell me how to look and talk. They ain't supposed to be hirin' me for what I look like – it's supposed to be for what I know and how I work. If they don't like my long hair, then they can find somebody else!" Well... they will, don't worry.

There was a television show several years ago on how a private group of educators decided that they were going to take several (about ten) guys from the ghetto of some large city and get them jobs. These guys were always complaining that they couldn't get jobs – that no one wanted to hire them. The first day of the meeting the instructors told them that they guaranteed jobs for them, but that they would have to do everything they were instructed during the five week training and preparation period. I think they lost two or three people right there because they, "Weren't going to have anyone tell them how to act and what to do." Wow, I wonder what they thought someone was going to pay them for – to come to work and not follow instructions?

The first thing they all had to do was to show up at the next meeting wearing a white shirt and tie – because to get a job they were told that first impressions are very important, and that what you wear, and the effort you make to get a job gives the interviewer an idea of your attitude and work ethic. It took about four more meetings before they all (except one guy) would actually show up with a white shirt and tie. The one guy finally showed up with a blue shirt and tie, and the instructor said, "No, I said a white shirt!" The guy quit the program because he just couldn't do what someone else instructed him to do.

How you talk can definitely matter too. I can't remember the statistics, but I recall reading a study that concluded that people that talked with a southern accent or drawl were automatically perceived by others to have a lower IQ. Now, why is that? I mean, I love the sound of a southern drawl. In fact, I am from the Midwest City of Dayton, Ohio – I mean Daaaytun, Ohiaaa. I'm not sure why, but I always made a concerted effort to limit my Midwest drawl, even in high school, but I'm sure people from the east coast detect it.

I think maybe the colloquial drawls of the areas throughout the U.S. are really not that important in searching for jobs unless the job is a management position that requires good verbal and written skills. If you want such a job, then it will probably be necessary for you to talk proper English. What is proper English, some say? We all know what it is. We have been taught it every year from about the third grade up through high school. Sometimes it amazes me how people are in denial of knowing proper English.

I understand that when we live among the colloquial Midwestern towns that it is acceptable to use improper English. I mean people use "them" people (instead of "those"), we "seen" (instead of "saw"), etc. As far as I'm concerned that's ok. Hey, I do a little of it myself from time to time. The problem is that when people need to use proper English they deny it. They say, "That's the way everyone talks around here – it's the standard."

Here's a test for you. Listen to your local newscasters on TV and the radio. You will find out they don't talk with any colloquial drawl. I use to travel all over the Midwest and the east and west coast from time to time, and I noticed that no matter what city and state I was in that the local television newscasters spoke proper English with minimal drawl or accent. It didn't matter if it was West Virginia, Tennessee, Chicago or Boston. Try noticing it once the next time you go traveling.

I do have a pet peeve concerning proper English. It is the use of the word "can" in place of the work "may." You know, "Can I help you?" We have all been taught through elementary and high school that in such usage the word "can" means – "am I able to." I know people aren't really asking me if they are able to help me because I have no idea as to their abilities. "May I help you," on the other hand asks the question, "Will you allow me to assist you.

Now people do the same thing with words such as "could" and "would" – You know, "Could you pass me the potatoes?" Yes, I could, now "would" you like me to? For years I have been noting when the phrase, "Can I help you is used instead of "May I help you," and I am sorry to report that only a few times have I heard: "May I help you?" It doesn't matter if I'm calling an attorney's office, a state government office, a large corporation, etc.; the telephone receptionist gets it wrong. It amazes me that at least one company or organization might realize that the improper use of an initial salutation from a representative of their organization may matter to the first impression of that organization.

This leads me to the subject of First Impressions. Most of what follows was extracted from an article overview by Jill Bremer entitled: "The Power of First Impressions." Ms. Bremer owns Bremer Communications which offers training, consulting and coaching in professional image development, communication and presentation skills. Some of her clients include Oracle, Abbott Labs, W.W. Grainger, U.S. Department of Energy and the National Association of Realtors. Most of what she says is not new or rocket science, but it is interesting and it is so much a part of human nature.

> "First impressions count! Packaging is important, whether we're considering a house, a product or a person. We think what looks attractive or reliable from the outside must surely be on the inside. We

judge books by their covers; we buy houses based upon curb appeal and we take people at face value. And they do the same to us!

I'll agree with you that none of this seems fair. People should be judged by their inner values and beliefs, but it is often the first impression that determines whether someone will stick around long enough for you to reveal those wonderful qualities. Very few people will ever see those documents that define who you are, such as your resume, diploma or birth certificate. Like it or not, it is often that first impression that determines your future, more than your professional achievements, family background or educational credentials.

When you step into a room, people make subconscious decisions about you. Within about thirty seconds, they've judged your economic and educational levels, your social position and your levels of sophistication and success. And keep in mind that they're basing those decisions purely upon what they see, i.e. your wardrobe, hairstyle, smile and posture.

After about four minutes, they've also made decisions about your trustworthiness, compassion, reliability, intelligence, capability, humility, friendliness and confidence. At this point you've probably had the opportunity to speak, so they're now taking into account the way your voice sounds, the content of what you say and how you say it.

Impressions are based upon instinct and emotion, not on rational thought or in-depth investigation. They are the product of the associations we make between outward characteristics and the inner qualities we believe they reflect. In other words, we filter everything we see and hear through our own experiences and biases and assign a stereotype to them. First impressions are a kind of human shorthand."[5]

First impressions are much like negative statements. By that I mean we can say all the wonderful, supportive and positive compliments we can to someone, but if we say one negative thing that is the one thing they will remember most. It is truly amazing how much we can improve our chances in succeeding in this world by being cognizant of human behavior.

"Are first impressions lasting impressions? Yes, for a couple of reasons. First, our life experience has taught us that our first impressions of others have usually been correct. And when these subconscious judgments were reinforced again and again, we grew to trust and believe in our instincts.

First impressions are also lasting because we hate to admit we make mistakes, so we cling to our opinions rather than revise them. Psychologists tell us that, once we apply a stereotype to someone, we spend the rest of our days seeking to validate it. Our rational brain kicks in and looks for every opportunity to confirm what the emotional side, with all of its biases and stereotypes, originally believed. That's not to say that negative first impressions can't be overcome, but it will take much time and effort. Remember that you're trying to overcome human nature and that's not an easy task."[5]

"When we talk of stereotypes, we instantly think of race or gender. But we all harbor assumptions

> regarding almost every human trait imaginable: tall or short, heavy or thin, articulate or not, clean or dirty, well mannered or rude, organized or disorganized. Whether we like to admit it or not, we all believe that one trait is preferable to another."[5]

If we are pursuing any endeavor that has some interface with people (and just about every endeavor will), then it is imperative that we know how people are going to view us. In sales it is a known fact that customers buy products mainly because they like or trust the salesman. People want to feel secure with the people in which they are dealing.

I recently heard a commentary on Walter Reed by Paul Harvey – you know, "The Rest of the Story." Supposedly, Walter Reed (the same one that the Army Medical Center is named after) was a brilliant scholar and doctor. In fact, I believe he was the youngest man to become a doctor (age 17, I think). He had a problem though – he couldn't make a go of his own medical practice. Why? - Because he couldn't grow facial hair well enough for a beard. You see, in those days almost every man wore a beard, and it was almost required to have one if a man was to be respected. He ended up going it research instead. Of course, he became a renowned doctor later in life, and was involved in the successful treatment of Yellow Fever.

This reminds me of when I became Superintendent of Wastewater Systems at a large county where I lived. I was thirty-four years old at the time. I have always worn a mustache because I like it, but also because it made me look older (that's what I thought anyway – I looked young for my age).

The position I held managed 85 people, including Plant Managers, Supervisors and Foremen. One of the technical staff was an older man (we'll call John) in his late sixties. He had been the Laboratory Technician that had helped me along as a new technician ten years earlier.

Since that time I had obtained my Masters degree, worked as Superintendent at an adjacent (smaller) county (for 4 years), and had obtained the highest license available.

I had been recruited back over to the larger county as Plant Manager of a very large, new facility. After a year I moved into the Superintendent position over all county treatment facilities. It was, perhaps, a little awkward for some people since some of the Supervisors and Plant Managers under me had been people in positions above me ten years earlier.

Never burn your bridges.

I believe that John was perhaps either a little jealous or just couldn't accept me in the position of Superintendent.

Note

It is very difficult to move up the ladder at some jobs because people in the workplace tend to always see you as the position you originally held. They pigeonhole you into a certain level, and it is difficult to break that mindset (breaking first impressions). Many times it is easier to hire some unknown person from the outside.

John was a sharp guy, but he was very opinionated, and would voice it when the need arose. There was one incident when I was in my office and heard him yelling at someone down the hall. He was using some profanity, and it was definitely getting out of hand. I emerged from my office and broke it up, and asked John to come into my office. I told him I wouldn't tolerate such emotional outbursts, etc. – in a very diplomatic and tactful way, of course (I am such a nice guy). After he left the office and was down the hall a ways I heard him say, "Damn baby-faced Superintendent!"

Boy, I went a long way to get to that didn't I?

I remember reading an article that said for the most part upper management jobs go to people in their forties. Regardless of one's education and experience there appears to be an unspoken age requirement. Of course, this is a general statement. There will always be exceptions. And, we are talking about management within an established business. There will always be a number of Bill Gates (Microsoft) and Steven Jobs (Apple Computer) around who start up their own business empires.

So, if you are young, well-educated, experienced and qualified for a position but get over-looked, don't take it personal, your day will come.

So, why are we the way we are in this respect? Have people always been quick to compartmentalize and classify people? Well, I'm sure the answer is "yes," but it could be that people in today's society are even better at such quick analyses of others.

> "Part of the problem is that we have no time today to make informed decisions. We have become a transient society, leading fast-paced lives with sound-bite mentalities. Our encounters with others are brief and lack substance. So we've come to believe "what we see is what we'll get". I believe television is largely the culprit. Television creates stereotypes and reinforces them constantly. It's also conditioned us to expect messages to be delivered

in thirty seconds. To prove my point, try watching a commercial, TV show or full-length movie without the sound. You can easily determine the characters and plot just by watching them. Analyzing the visual messages from their clothing, behavior and body language is all you need to understand the relationships and story lines.

So what can we do to be in control of how others perceive us? Confucius said, *"In all things, success depends upon preparation, and without such preparation, there is sure to be failure."* All you have to do is to decide who your audience will be in any given situation, determine your objectives and make choices that match the audience's expectations. Do you want the promotion, the recognition, the relationship? Whatever your objectives may be, decide what qualities the decision-maker expects from that type of person and then dress, behave and communicate in the expected way.

Take a cue from successful salespeople. They employ a technique called "mirroring". They know that when they reflect the posture, speaking style and wardrobe of the other party, they open the lines of communication. That person begins to see them as someone who understands them and who shares their same values. Trust is quickly built and the deal is sealed. Try the same technique yourself. Think ahead to your objectives each day and whom you will encounter. Make choices that reflect their style of dress, behavior and communication and watch what happens!"[5]

Well, it's fun to think we are unique in how we look, communicate and generally project ourselves, but it's unfortunate that some people never get the picture that to get where we want to go we must all conform to some standards of first impressions. I guess if you bought some land up in the Canadian tundra and lived your life out among the animals you could make it not conforming, but that's about the only place.

We can all do ourselves a favor and evaluate our lives, prioritize our desires, and adapt accordingly. It's much easier to change things from the inside than it is from the outside, and if you are at the top, then you have more power. So, instead of whining about conformities at one's job or workplace, he/she should concentrate on doing what it takes to move up and have more control over such changes. Or, start his/her own business.

Chapter 4 - Getting Started

Gosh, we're almost halfway through the book, and we have yet to discuss the mechanics and structure of how to do all this endeavor determination and ISO program implementation. That's a good thing, though, because it means it won't take long, and it will be easy!

As discussed previously, we have a better chance at removing mind clutter if we do a little self-introspection to determine what we should really be devoting our brain to. We can't just pick something to focus on without some serious consideration. If psychologists are correct, and our human makeup drives us to be "all that we can be" it makes sense that we should take some time to determine what exactly it is that we want to be or do with our life.

When I was in the process of writing this book I remember discussing it with a friend and he said, "Oh, I already do goals. I set goals for myself all the time," he said. I said, "But I'm not talking about career goals, or family goals or financial goals or success goals. I'm talking about what you're supposed to do in life to be happy – life endeavors." I don't think he got it.

It may be clearer to some than it is to others. For example, if someone has an overwhelming talent, then developing that talent may probably be his/her primary endeavor in life. For the majority of us, however, it is not as easy to discern our true calling. Instead, we may jump from one thing to another thinking each is the most important. These things many times turn out to be just more and more diversion in the name of "crises management."

For instance, so many problems revolve around finances and the management of them that many people think this is the "root of all evil," and that a solution to money management is a solution to life happiness. There are hundreds of books to assist in organizing personal finances. Even this book has some money management ideas, but they will be simplified approaches. Finance is only one aspect of your life, and it is most likely not the primary aspect in managing your life.

> ☑ Don't expect money to bring you happiness.[1]

As further evidence to the need of real thought when developing endeavors, one person may say that family comes first. His or her happiness comes from the "American Dream" of having kids, a house, property, a good job and friends to spend time with. For others the job comes first. The competitive nature of succeeding in the business world brings great joy. To say these things are not important would be wrong, but we want to make sure that they are really things we want out of life, not things done out of expectation by others, guilt from society, or misplaced esteem "needs" within ourselves.

Note

Being able to properly prioritize activities in your life is very important. We all tend to operate in a "crisis management" approach. What does that mean? It means we have no real organized priority beyond focusing on whatever jerks our chain the most – usually those things that need to be done immediately.

Pre-existing Endeavors

Before we go through the process of determining our true-life endeavors we should look at what we think we already know about what we want. It would be a good time right now to write down what you think is important to you in life; before you read any further in this book.

Don't just jot down what you think is important currently, but include what endeavors, if any, you may have for yourself and your family or loved ones. If you haven't thought about any endeavors up to now, don't include any at this point. If your endeavors have been very general, like "raise the kids to be good citizens," or "live life to the fullest," or become the best violinist ever," etc., just jot these down. Don't start now to get specific if you haven't already. Making up a few endeavors without considerable thought at this point will not be beneficial.

Spend as much time as you feel is necessary. For some, it may take a few minutes. For others, it may take a lot longer. Many of you may have no endeavors at all. Please do it now, though, before you proceed on with this book. Once you have done this, just set it aside for now. We will use it later.

Time to Determine a Life Endeavor

So, first and foremost, we need to define our endeavors. Believe it or not, this initial step is commonly overlooked, or perhaps not acknowledged. By that I mean, we know what the endeavors are in our mind, but we never set them down on paper, or never dwell on them sufficiently enough to specifically define them.

The other problem is we tend to set endeavors for more than just ourselves. We set them in terms of the family, or in terms of the "good" of others. Ah yes, most of us were raised to put the welfare of others before ourselves. That is, we do things for our spouse, our kids, our parents, the less fortunate, our boss, the company, our friends, charity, etc. In reality, though, are we really doing things for others? Or, are we trying to please others in order to get recognition or attention for ourselves?

I come from a very musical family. Everyone plays an instrument. Although I loved to play basketball as a kid I also liked music. My dad is a super musician. He played piano, guitar, bass and trombone. I took piano lessons for a while then settled into the trombone and played it throughout high school. In college I took up the guitar, and enjoyed it. I ended up taking classical guitar lessons and practiced and played daily. I am 57 years old, and when dad comes over to visit I realize that a good part of the reason I play is to get his approval and appreciation. I am sure I also play to get applause from other people and words of praise and love from those close to me. So, I'm not necessarily playing for my own enjoyment, but for the attention I get from it.

In the ISO programs of industry they usually start off with a Policy consisting of Goals. I use the word "goal," but in reality the ISO programs and standards do not use the word "goal," but rather "policy." I'm sure it's because a "policy" is ongoing and a goal has a beginning and an end. For ISO 9000 the policy consists of desired "quality" in their product/s. These policies are carefully defined because all other parts of the ISO program are concerned with how these policies will be "achieved", how they will be "maintained, and how they will be improved." Once policies are defined then other elements of the ISO standards are adapted. These other elements include:

- *Planning* – This is where objectives and targets are defined that will assist in conforming to the policy.

- *Implementation* – This is where methods are defined by which to proceed; like what steps will be required to progress forward in conforming to the policy.

- *Checking* – This is where measurements are documented and interpreted constantly to monitor how things are going; that is, evaluating the ongoing program.

In setting your endeavors you must do some introspective, soul-searching. You must make sure that the endeavors are only directed towards your happiness; not others. Making other people happy does not usually count. Many people tend to think this (making others happy) makes them happy, but in reality it turns out that this gives people a sense of satisfaction towards service and duty to loved ones, friends and society.

Also, people may actually be performing such actions out of guilt. Guilt plays such a large part in the average American psyche. It is time to free yourself of guilt, and think about yourself, and your dreams. This whole process is personal and private. No one will know what you are thinking, just you. If it's any consolation, people that satisfy their own needs end up making the people around them happy anyway; funny how that works out.

Sometimes what appears to be an endeavor is actually a sub-goal to a larger, more important goal that you never considered. For example, maybe you think the accumulation of money will set you free to be yourself. It's true that this may allow you do a lot of things you never had the opportunity to do, but what you need to do is assume money is no object. Now, what would you do to be happy?

One person may say they would buy a restaurant, and make it the best in the world. Another would say they would give much of their money away; maybe for a new house for their parents, etc. Be careful, such a desire is not about you directly. This is not about what you would do if you had all the money in the world. Maybe it would be better to assume that you have all the money you will ever need, and all the relatives are wealthy due to your generosity, and you have given to all the charities, etc. Now, what would you do?

"Well, gee," you say? "I always wanted to play the piano, but I'm way too old to do that now." Now, you are getting closer to what will make you personally happy.

Remember, it is unlikely that you will have all the money in the world to help all the people you want to (or to relieve all your guilt). Besides, it is not your duty or responsibility to solve everyone's problems. You do, however, have a very good chance at acquiring money or budgeting your money in order to accomplish your endeavor/s for happiness. You will see.

Once you have defined a direction, an endeavor, and a plan you will be surprised how you will be able to accumulate the resources needed to make it happen. Don't stop spending a dollar a week on the lotto, though. I don't encourage planning your future on luck or gambling, but an insignificant investment with high possible gain maybe can't hurt. Such a luck-driven "long shot" always provides some possibility for unexpected surprises. Now, let's get back to reality.

To help you along in thinking about endeavors, I have included examples of three different people. We will follow these people through the method of setting endeavors, as well as the rest of the process. The situation of each is different. You may identify with one of the examples, but the exercises provide alternative ways of thinking; so, you will get something out of each scenario.

1. **Sam Single** – Sam is a single person in his late twenties. He has never been married, but has had several girlfriends, and has experienced the pain of breaking up as well as the joy of love. The trouble is, although Sam is a good worker, he can't seem to save enough money to get out of the routine of living from paycheck to paycheck. He never went to college or trade school after high school. He is tired of working hard, but still depending upon infrequent financial help from his parents and friends. He wants to feel secure and independent.

2. **Howard Hitched** – Howard is a married man with two teenage boys. Howard is well educated and makes an attractive income of just under six figures. His wife is formally educated too, but has not taken advantage of her education and experience because she has been a mother to the children. Even though Howard makes a good income he has not been able to save much for retirement, and he has a lot of upcoming expenses with college for the boys. He loves his family and "being a father," but he is becoming concerned that he is just "living to work," not "working to live."

3. **Tracy Trapped** – Tracy is a woman in her mid forties. She is married, and not happy because her every move is controlled by her husband. She has been married before, and entered into her current marriage because her husband had a child with a physical disability, and Tracy has great compassion for children. In fact, she brought two of her own children from her previous marriage to live as part of the new family. Her husband owns several small businesses and projected the appearance of security to Tracy when she met him. What she didn't know was that he was a control fanatic. He is jealous of her good looks, and he never lets her leave the home on her own. Although, he generates a very good income, Tracy loves working at the nearby factory, and has made a good income of her own there; in fact that's where they met. Her income and other inherited monies; however, have gone straight to her husband who manages all budget and income. She has to ask for spending money, and has to

> be very frugal in her spending. She is trapped
> because if she leaves him, she fears he will
> retain parental rights over his disabled daughter,
> and Tracy knows that would be disastrous.

You should be thinking about your happiness. It may take a while, and you should consider all the pros and cons of each endeavor you evaluate. Make two lists next to each other. List the potential endeavor at the top, and then list all the pros of pursuing the endeavor on one side of the paper, and all the cons on the other side. As you do this keep thinking about each. Put the list down for a while and then pick it up at a later time. Take your time. Also, if you think better at a certain time of the day consider doing your thinking then.

I think better in the morning, and am sleepy or less attentive in the afternoon and evening. I do all my writing and thinking in the morning, and all my phoning, talking and visiting later in the day.

If you have problems with writing or seeing to write, buy an audio recorder. There are all kinds of pocket, hand held units that digitally record large amounts of information, and you can skip to different points in memory instantly like a CD player. Of course, there are mini and micro tape hand held units too. While you are mulling over your endeavors, read through the scenarios of the three example people. It may give you some ideas.

It is important to realize that, as people, we are constantly changing. We become smarter with the things we learn each day, and we become wiser with age. Our "likes and "dislikes" also change with our age, and so will our endeavors to some degree. I say this because in defining endeavors that make you happy, you should be aware that someday down the road you may have to do this all over again; some more frequently than others. I don't mean your endeavors will necessarily "completely" change, but they may need some modification for the "change in times." Or, you may need to do the process again to reinforce or re-confirm your thoughts.

Chapter 5 - Sam's Endeavor

As stated in the short bio of Sam provided earlier, he is a young man who wants to get a hold on his life. He needs some direction. He is tired of just "living life," and not achieving happiness. Sam sat down and looked seriously at his situation. He had worked for more than six years at a hotel. He began as a worker at banquet setup, and then became dayshift team leader. He also gained experience as a bar back and then bartender. He also became a busboy and then waiter at the hotel's restaurant. He is a self-taught guitar player and had been the leader of a local alternative-rock band. He had held other jobs in manufacturing and fast food restaurants. One commonality of all the jobs was that he had a good work ethic, and people liked him. We won't go into a psychological analysis of Sam, but he did come from a divorced family situation where his parents split up when he was sixteen years old.

Sam did not do well all through high school, but his aptitude test indicated he was smarter than the level at which his performance indicated. He developed a very low self-esteem, and he felt music was the only real thing he was good at. Even when his parents tried to convince him to try college or trade school, he shunned it off because he didn't think he was smart enough. He wanted to be able to budget his income better, but convinced himself he couldn't do the math, even when his parents attempted to help him learn and provided simple accounting budget methods.

He applied the self-introspection technique to evaluate just what he wanted out of life. He looked at marriage and family. Yes, he thought at some point that was something he would like to do. When he really thought about it, he determined that he did want the love and companionship of a woman, and he didn't like being lonely. However, he figured that the reason he would have children was because his wife undoubtedly would want them. So, it wasn't so much his desire to have a family, but more that he expected the woman he married would want to. He wasn't ruling out that his desires may change in the future, but he just knew for now this is how he felt. So, when he looked at this in view of Maslow's hierarchy of needs, the wife and family were not his self-actualization. Maslow says we must have the second and third level of needs met before we can proceed to self-actualization.

The fact that Sam was struggling with saving money indicates he is still trying to satisfy some of the "Safety" needs of level two. And, the fact that he has identified the need for love and companionship indicates that he is feeling the needs of level three, "Belonging and Love." He concluded that a wife and family were more of a "condition" he would like to live in (not alone), rather than what "personally" would make him happy in life.

Note

See, having some general awareness of information like Maslow's Hierarchy of Needs, can help us to not misinterpret "needs" as "endeavors."

In the back of his mind, Sam always thought that he wanted to really pursue a music career. That is, he wanted to pursue one of the American dreams of becoming a rock star. That seemed to bring fame, money and women. He thought carefully about it, and knew he would have to put some real effort into getting better at the guitar. He couldn't read music, and he had seen so many extremely good guitarists that he would have to compete with that he just knew it would take some real effort. If not, he could stay in the groove he was in of getting by with playing at an intermediate level and singing. He wasn't too bad looking, but he also wasn't getting any younger, and the rock star age group was fast departing him; or he was departing it? Since he didn't feel the urge to get started doing what it takes to be a good technical instrumentalist on the guitar, he decided that must not be his real passion. He must have been doing it mostly for the attention he derived from it, or for the personal esteem needs it provided.

Note

This is a good point. One test of whether something is really of interest to you is to think about how willing you are to put in the effort to do whatever it is to be the best.

When I was young I lived to play basketball. I went over to my friend's house every single day after school to play on his large driveway court. I chipped ice in the winter and played in heavy coats and gloves. This was my love. In the same way, my brother practiced the piano for hours, even as a small child. When people hear how wonderfully my brother plays the piano they ask my mom, "Did it take a lot to make him practice?" She always answered, "Are you kidding? We had to make him quit. He would practice into the night while we were trying to sleep."

So, if what you think will make you happy the rest of your life is creating or performing, think about how happy it makes you to prepare (practice) your craft. If it's a drag, then it probably is not what makes you happy, but rather you are inherently good at it; so, you may feel you are supposed to do it. I wonder how many tall boys went into playing basketball because of their height?

So, now Sam decided to think about other careers and interests he has had over the years. First, he thought about his experience in the job market. Most of it had been associated with food service of some sort. He really feels comfortable with hotel and restaurant management and service. Back when he was working in that area he used to feel he could run his own place. He had visions of operating a small bar or coffee house where his music buddies could come and perform. He had experience in sound engineering and lighting. Of course, he just daydreamed about it because there was no way he could ever afford to buy such a place.

Now, his thoughts on such an establishment had changed. Lately, he had envisioned owning more of a café restaurant where he could host the customers, perform some guitar himself, and have visiting performers come in. It would be a quieter, more relaxed, upscale atmosphere. The more he thought about it, the more he knew that it was something that really interested him. The problem was the expense and regulations, and just all the unknowns. He just never really considered it.

He was reminded that in this process of defining what makes us happy we are to assume we have all the money, and means. We are not to concern ourselves with the "how" at anytime when developing endeavors. We are dreaming and only our dreams will reveal what we really want. "Ok," says Sam. "That's it. I want to own a café or restaurant. But there's no way that will ever happen." Ok, Sam, let's worry about the "how" later.

Sam, you have now defined what will make you happy. Next, write down all the things that are exciting about the endeavor. For example, Sam started talking about how he would be his own boss, how he would get to see the expression of delightfulness on his customers' faces as he provided the best service possible. He thought of the fun it would be to perform and to have performers visit. He knew the reason people liked him was that he enjoyed the interface with people, and this too would be a benefit to owning his own restaurant. He went on and on. "Write it down, Sam"

Note

Sam is visualizing. Remember how visualizing plays such an important part in "selling" and "preparing" oneself?

PERSONAL ENDEAVOR DETERMINATION					
Marriage & Family		**Guitar Player**		**Cafe/Restaurant**	
Pros	*Cons*	*Pros*	*Cons*	*Pros*	*Cons*
-Need love and companionship	-Assuming wife will want kids, but not me now	-I really enjoy playing the guitar, and playing in a band	-There is a lot of competition in guitar playing	-I would be able to perform at my own place	-I don't know all the regulations concerning the food business
	-This is more of a living condition than a personal endeavor	-I am good at playing the guitar, and it is probably one of the few things I can do well	-Cannot read music, and there are so many more better players than me	-I always liked the service environment, and get a lot of enjoyment out of meeting and pleasing people	-I don't have the money to start such a venture
		-I enjoy the attention I get from people in performing	-I would need to really spend a lot of time to become the best guitar player possible	-I feel comfortable (with my experience) in managing my own place	
			-I don't think I have the patience or desire to put in all the practice needed to compete	-I could have other performers perform, and would get to see and hear them myself	
				-I like music sound systems, and have experience with them in live entertainment	
				-I have always enjoyed cooking, and trying new menu items	
Endeavor Resolution					
Owning my own café/restaurant where I can have live music and good service seems very exciting. I love cooking, and I love meeting people, and serving them. I'll get to perform, and to have others that I choose perform.					

94

Chapter 6 - Howard's Endeavor

Howard may be the most common example of the three. He has a good job, and he has a great family. From all outward appearances he looks to be happy and normal. He does work a lot, and so sometimes feels that he is "living to work" instead of "working to live." He is in his late forties, and has been thinking about what will happen when he retires in the not-too-distant future. He remembers back when he first got married, and both he and his wife were working full time. She had a good accounting position with a large firm. He remembers thinking that together they would be able to generate enough income to retire early and do some traveling. That was the plan. Now, twenty-some years later things didn't seem to turn out the way he had planned.

Remember that great line from the movie "The Natural?" Roy Hobbs was a naturally gifted baseball player that was recruited into the major leagues right out of high school. His plan was simple – "to be the best baseball player there ever was." But on the train trip to the majors something happened that interrupted his life for sixteen years; something he never planned on. To find out what it was watch the movie. The point here is that when he meets up with his long lost true love sixteen years later she says, "What happened to you Roy?" His answer, "Things didn't turn out the way I thought they would."

Now, Howard is thinking the same thing. "What happened?" Let's see, the kids came along, and he and his wife didn't really think about the money it takes to raise them. They just knew they wanted kids. And with the kids they needed to move to a bigger house and to a community where the kids would get the best education possible. Then, there were the toys and accessories. Of course, Howard had to take up playing golf because he wanted to be part of the management team at work; that was an unexpected expense. His wife too needed extra curricular activities. Raising kids is not for sissies someone once said.

All in all, they were living the American dream of a big house in the suburbs, the kids and the toys to go along. Unfortunately, it seems that part of the American dream is to live from paycheck to paycheck, and not worry about saving money for the future - there's his retirement plan, and social security, after all. Now, he reads about how the social security system may not stay in tact, and with the major economic recession his retirement portfolio is no way nearly sufficient.

Howard's mind is becoming cluttered with thoughts of "what should have happened," and desperate thoughts of "how will I get out of this situation." He's beginning to have thoughts of "jumping ship" and relieving his burden of perceived responsibility. Howard needs to stop, and figure it out. He needs to determine what will make him happy, and to manage all parts of his life.

Note

You may notice that I don't usually consider better money management as an endeavor to happiness. Managing money is a problem for almost everyone. Everyone knows they need to be proactive in saving money and preparing for down times, job loss, unexpected maintenance, etc. The problem is, it is like dieting or quitting smoking; without proper motivation it is very difficult. People tend to keep putting it off, and rationalizing it by telling themselves that "life is too short," and they need to live life to the fullest.

Fulfillment and happiness just doesn't come from doing and buying things to fill up our lives. They just don't last. Buying a car is a good example. When someone goes out to buy a car they fall in love with the color, or the make, or body style or the projected image. It seems real important at the time. Then, about six months to a year later it just becomes another vehicle. All those important reasons to buy that particular car seem to fade away. When an individual has a true endeavor, then he/she has the motivation to lose the weight, save the money, etc.

It became time for Howard to do some soul-searching, and in-depth self-introspection to determine what would make him happy.

Now, I should interject here that we are following Howard as an example. In real life, his wife should also determine her happiness endeavor, and the two should then plan to attain them together. For the sake of brevity, I have decided to concentrate just on Howard.

Howard considered the activities of his life. First, he thought about his job. He liked it ok, but he was looking forward to retiring because it was taking up too much of his time. He knew it wasn't that he enjoyed doing the job so much as that it came easy for him after all these years of working. In fact, he had become so good at what he did that he had gone out on his own (started his own business) providing contracting services to industrial clients about ten years earlier. In any event, he ruled out any interest related to his job as being related to self-actualization.

Next, he thought about golf. He really liked golf, but he wasn't that good. He wasn't a natural athlete or anything, and he knew no matter how hard he would practice that he would never compete at an advanced level. He thought about golf as I suggested; that is, did he want to spend the time at golf to be the best? Heck, no. Golf was just a way to meet clients and relax in a beautiful environment; nothing wrong with that.

How about the activities surrounding golf? Did he want to work part-time at the clubhouse? Did being around the people and activities really interest him? Not really. He liked going there to eat dinner with friends and family, but beyond that he would just as leave stay home.

What about other hobbies such as woodworking, artwork, playing a musical instrument, etc.? He couldn't think of any that he had ever really had much desire to do. So, if he had idle time to himself, what did he do, or want to do? He liked dining out with friends. He liked traveling. Should he start a new career as a Travel Agent? Nah! No way he wanted to deal with people and their needs all day.

Hey, there was something he had forgotten. He loved to trade stocks; or rather he would love to be able to trade stocks. He had money in a retirement SEP account that he originally had in a mutual fund through his insurance company. He had transferred a small part of it to an on-line SEP account where he could actually buy and sell stocks from his computer. He could watch the stocks change in real time using his own streamer of portfolio stocks. He also watched one of the stock channels on cable TV almost every morning, and while working he kept a watch on his account when he had the chance.

He had never considered it something he could do in retirement or as a pastime because he just didn't have that much money in the account; and it takes money to make money. Also, the stock market had been in a steep decline for almost three years now, and making any significant money didn't seem possible. But as he thought about it, he did really enjoy learning about all the stocks, and he had his own ideas on what types to buy and what to trade. Even in a declining bear market there were always many stocks moving upward, and he had a knack for finding them. He had been watching and learning for about three years.

"What was it that he enjoyed about trading stocks," he thought? He liked the idea that he was his own boss, that he could make moneymaking decisions on his own, and reap the profits or the losses. He liked the "potential" for significant profit taking. He remembers one day back three years ago when the market was bullish that he had made $3,000 in just one trade. He bought shares of a stock at 10:00 am and sold them at 11:30 am and immediately made $3,000. At the time he thought to himself, "how much time and effort would I put into getting a client to buy my services, and at the sales percentage what would I make." He thought, "I made more money in an hour and a half than I could in two weeks of working with a client. Not only that, look at the paperwork and reports I would have to write for the client."

Another thing he liked about trading stocks was the fact that he could work out of his home. He could wear his home clothes, or his pajamas for that matter. Just think, he could come and go as he pleased. Maybe trade for a while, and then go out and about. He could schedule trips and go whenever he desired. The more he thought about it, the more he got excited. But then, he remembered. He would need more money to sustain a living and to bring his retirement savings up to where it needed to be.

Just hold on Howard! Remember, we aren't concerned with the "how," but only the "what." You have defined your endeavor, now make a list of the things you just thought about and keep reinforcing your endeavor with more pros. Don't forget the cons too, because cons are listed in order to turn them into pros. To see an example of what I mean about listing the pros and cons, see Sam Single's previous section.

Chapter 7 - Tracy's Endeavor

Tracy is not an example of the average person. She was unaware of her husband's true nature when she entered into her current marriage. Now she feels she is trapped without a way out. This is not an example of a married couple having disagreements or normal marital problems. It is a case where the husband is causing mental abuse through extreme control. Tracy is belittled routinely, and made to feel more like a slave than a wife.

By using this example, I am not proposing that people having difficulties in their marriage should give up or rationalize an extreme solution. In general, all marriages have problems, and a great many need the assistance of a marriage counselor at least once during their duration. Please just accept, for this example, that this is a special case of abuse. However, be aware that these cases of abuse definitely exist everywhere in the world.

The reason Tracy feels trapped is because her husband's daughter, Carina, has a physical disability that has hindered her development and social interaction. Tracy "lives" to help her out. Tracy has always been good with children. In a former marriage she even ran a childcare business from her home.

Tracy also has a very good built-in support group in her brother and sisters. They all know the situation, and help her to bear the depression and helplessness she feels. Her brother and sisters all live out of state and far away; so, she doesn't get the needed time with them. Tracy knows she could leave at anytime and stay with her sisters, but she has three teenage girls (including Carina) living with her. She is so afraid that if she left her husband that Carina would probably be forced to live with her father, and Tracy just couldn't bear that. Her brother and sisters have told her that since Carina is 15 years old; that she is of age to be able to stay with whatever parent she chooses. The problem is that Carina is not adopted by Tracy, and Tracy knows the power and control her husband has. He would hire the best attorneys, and make it difficult. Tracy just doesn't want to uproot the girls now during these sensitive high school years.

Tracy needs a plan. She needs to tap her resources. She has good factory job experience; so, she knows she could get a factory job if she needed to. She is a gifted artist, but doesn't see how this is of any help. She has the help of her brother and sisters, should she need support or temporary living quarters.

She has thought many times that if she could just make it until Carina was 18 years old, then she could leave, and Carina would be at legal age to live on her own or with whomever she decided. So, although "getting away" is not a personal happiness endeavor, it is something that needs to happen if Tracy is going to be able to make it mentally. And she really needs to determine an endeavor, and know that she is working toward it all the time. You see, just having a plan can provide resolution to a difficult situation. It can help one make it through such times even if the plan never, actually transpires.

This may be a case where a person, perhaps, should not concentrate on her self-actualization, but rather on her mental health. Maslow would say Tracy still has basic needs she can't acquire under her current life conditions, they are:

- **Safety and Security** – Tracy continually has to deal with fear of abuse.

- **Belonging & Love** – This powerful need for someone to love is not fulfilled.

- **Esteem** – Belittlement via mental abuse results in lack of esteem for Tracy.

Still, to obtain these needs it will be beneficial for her to think about what she would really like to do with her life. It will be very difficult for her because worries over abuse and security tend to keep her mind pre-occupied. Instead, she dreams of a time when she can be free, but it is just that – a dream.

In our scenario, Tracy does decide to do some deep soul searching in order to determine what would make her happy. First, she has to accept a few conditions. One, she has to assume she is independently wealthy. Second, she has to assume Carina has reached the age of 18, and is doing well on her own. Finally, she has to assume that she has the independence to do whatever she wants.

She also has to think about all the things she would do when she is free that she always wanted to do - things like going shopping, going dancing, meeting new friends, fixing up a place of her own, visiting her sisters, etc. These are all important things she wants to do, but if she has all the money and time to do these things, will that be what ultimately satisfies her? No, these are just things she has missed. More accurately they are things associated with the safety, love and esteem needs that have not been met.

Once she has identified all these things, then she needs to accept that she has had the opportunity to do them, and feel good about life. Now, she needs to determine what she, personally, needs to do to make herself happy (i.e. self-actualization). I just hope she doesn't fixate at one of the levels of needs.

It may be note-worthy to remember that Maslow indicated that many times people who have endured extreme hardship or experienced catastrophic conditions many times "fixate" at a certain needs level.

> "If you have significant problems along your development – a period of extreme insecurity or hunger as a child, or the loss of a family member through death or divorce, or <u>significant neglect</u> <u>or abuse</u> – <u>you may</u> <u>"fixate" on that set of needs for the rest of your life</u>."

> "This is Maslow's understanding of neurosis. Perhaps you went through a war as a kid. Now you have everything your heart desires – yet you still find yourself obsessing over having enough money and keeping the pantry well-stocked. Or perhaps your parents divorced when you were young. Now you have a wonderful spouse – yet you get insanely jealous or worry constantly that they are going to leave you because you are not "good enough" for them."[3].

Note

Tracy may end up with some lasting problems related to this. If she remains in this environment of control and repression, she may never get "enough" freedom when she gets on her own. That is to say, a permanent and long-term relationship with another man may be very difficult for her. The makeup and character of each person is different; so, there is no way of telling. If she is aware of this possibility though, (through information like Maslow's works) then she may have a better chance of recognizing these needs and better dealing with them. The longer a person stays in a life situation (even abusive) the harder it will be to get out of it. People tend to keep rationalizing their lack of change because it is stressful to make such changes. Under abusive or uncomfortable living conditions people many times acquire their satisfaction or personal needs through others; such as their children's lives. This is really not a long term fulfillment, but the mind has a way of dealing with adverse situations in its own way. I urge people to take their lives into their own hands, and don't let it waste away.

Ok, at this point Tracy starts listing things in her mind. She always wanted to go back to college. She had taken a few courses in her early years, but it was interrupted by the needs of others (i.e. her husband, her children, etc.). What is it she liked about school? Well, she always wanted to be smarter. She had always been attracted to intelligent people. The more she thought about it, however, the more she thought, perhaps, at the time it was a way to get out and meet people. She loved to meet people, and she loved to have fun. Perhaps it wasn't that she really had some specific interest or subject she wanted to learn more about, but more that she wanted to feel better about herself. For the moment, she decided to look at other things. The school thing seemed a little non-specific. Maybe she would get back to thoughts on it later.

Note

> This is a good idea, by the way. If you seem to be at a dead-end thinking about a possible endeavor, just make some notes about what you have thought about it, and go on to another aspect of your endeavor search.

Tracy thought about another love of her life – art. She was a talented artist, and did some very impressive drawings when she was younger. She just never had the opportunity to do any such creative ventures while she was a mother and wife. She did do a lot of interior design of her house, and was always changing, rearranging and redesigning the house. She also loved working out in her big yard. She loved flowers and gardens and landscaping. She was not afraid to get her hands dirty and work hard to create a beautiful flower garden. So, should she try and recapture her artistic ability of painting and drawing? What kind of money could she make doing that, though? Whoops! She forgot that she is not to be concerned with money when determining what makes her happy. She'll figure that out later.

This was very difficult for her to discern. She would just be happy to be free, and not be controlled. Tracy decided to evaluate her three potential interests a little further. She wrote down all the pros and cons of each. Concerning school, she knew getting additional education would make her feel better about herself. Also, it would definitely add to her tools in getting a different kind of job, other than in a factory. Of course, she thought it would be fun mingling with a new crowd of people – people that were perhaps more interesting.

When she thought about becoming an artist, she knew she loved to be creative, and to draw and paint, but she wondered if she could really be happy putting in the effort to make a life of it. It is a rather personal and independent career. She probably wouldn't get the interaction with people that her personality really desired.

Then, she considered interior and exterior decorating. It was still a creative outlet, and it gave her opportunity to be both inside and outside. It was also something that involved more interaction with people. Something else appealed to her about this option. She could do it on her own, and make a business of it. She was very familiar with how to run a business such as this because one of the businesses her husband owned was a construction and truck-hauling business. She did much of the bookkeeping, and answered the phones, etc.; so, she felt very comfortable with the thought of owning a business.

As she thought more about it, she could go back to school and get a degree in interior design, and also take courses on art to resurrect her drawing and painting skills. The degree would give her the credibility needed as an interior design business owner, and also satisfy her need to obtain more knowledge. All these things were very "people" oriented activities that she would enjoy.

Tracy made her lists of pros and cons. She thought more and more about it, and decided this was an exciting idea. This was to be what she would pursue.

Chapter 8 - Finishing Up Endeavors

I am assuming that by now you have defined your true lot in life, so to speak. Once you have your endeavor, and you have sufficiently thought it through (listing the pros and cons), compare it to the endeavor you jotted down before you started. Do they match those goals? Do you feel better about the new life endeavor? Are you ready to determine how to reach your life endeavor? You should be, you know. You live only once, you'll not get another chance at being all that you can be; and feeling the happiness of doing what you know is right (unless, of course, you believe in reincarnation). Everyone around you will be happier too because when you are happy you will make others happy.

Note

Nothing in life is perfect; so, if you're worried whether or not you have been able to identify your endeavor – just relax. I just wanted to make sure you took the time to give it some real thought. Regardless of whether you have defined your true endeavor or not – you are probably close enough.

Summary

In determining our life endeavors we need to give it as much thought as possible. This is where we are truly thinking about life, and how we fit in. The more we ponder this, the better we will feel about arriving at an endeavor. Don't forget, though, life is not perfect, and we may not arrive at an endeavor that just "stands out." That's ok because we need to focus on something throughout our life whether it is exactly right or not. We may have to change – flexibility and change is a part of life. The important thing is that we are clearing our minds of clutter and moving along in a direction throughout our lives.

Listed below are some things or "checks" you can ask yourself concerning the development of your endeavor that may keep you on track:

1. A test to see if it is our endeavor is to ask ourselves if we enjoy every aspect of it - like "practicing."

2. We need to ask ourselves if we want to do it out of guilt, obligation or attention – or if we are doing it strictly for ourselves. We should want to do it even if nobody else is around to appreciate it.

3. We should want to do it without any concern for whether or not it makes money.

4. It should generally give us a feeling of happiness or satisfaction to do it.

5. Make sure it's not a "need" – you know one of Maslow's needs? It may sound easy, but if we think about it needs are so easily confused with personal endeavors. The need for love and esteem are so strong. People get lonely and are fixated on trying to find their soul mate; that is, satisfying the need for love and belonging. So, when they think singing or playing the piano or

bodybuilding or writing poetry or becoming rich is their endeavor, it may in fact be their subconscious thinking this will attract the opposite sex, and that's why they are doing it. Or concerning self-esteem, they may be doing something to get attention or recognition (e.g. rock guitarist, race car driver, rich person, etc.). They may be still trying to acquire self-esteem from others by doing these things.

6. We want to make sure that we are not defining a goal instead of an endeavor. Remember, a goal has a beginning and an end, whereas an endeavor (like a program) is on-going. So things like reaching a certain management level or salary level is a goal. Making a sculpture of your loved one is a goal. Sculpturing the rest of your life is an endeavor.

All that I have talked about in this book most of you have probably had some exposure to – say in high school or college (as a psychology course) or in management training, reading books or magazines, etc. The beauty of this book is now we get to bring all these things together and think about them, and how they affect our lives. It helps us to be more confident because we feel we have really given it some thought – doesn't it? Thinking and dreaming is fun, isn't it? Just wait until you get to implement it!

Chapter 9 - Implementation

In identifying an approach to reaching our life endeavors we will want to make it as simple as possible. It will involve some bookkeeping and some routine checking of how we are doing; but we don't want to make it a "hassle." We want to make it so we can keep on track, and be motivated by our monitoring.

First, it is once again time to do some thinking; some introspection. As mentioned before, do not be afraid to think about this in a self-centered way. Do not worry about the impact it may have on others around you. Just think and jot down your ideas. Later you can revise and rethink your thoughts and determine a way they will not adversely impact others around you. It is so important to think about this thoroughly and consider all options.

Two of the most common obstacles to implementing a plan of action are "time" and "money," and they are interrelated. When planning any project or program the "how" and "when" are related to the availability of resources (money being the most significant resource). And many times the availability of resources is dependent on the time required to accumulate the resources. So, pursuing a life endeavor can many times be related to the time it will take to accumulate those resources.

Now the "time" is usually also related to other factors. For example, maybe other life circumstances have to be completed, or at least completed to a certain point before part or most of our plan can be implemented. We can't just "up and change everything that's going on." We must plan a way to "phase" our implementation into our daily lives. For instance, maybe paying off the mortgage, or paying for college expenses or paying off an auto loan, etc. will have to be completed before some or all of our plan can be implemented.

Remember, we have no time limit on pursuing any aspect of our endeavor. It is on-going until we die. Do not be impatient but, rather embrace the journey toward the endeavor (i.e. the process) because this is many times just as satisfying as performing the endeavor.

Chapter 10 - Planning

The first part of implementation is defining more accurately our endeavor and how we will achieve it. We will need to think about such things as:

- Financial Needs
- Chronology of Events
- Research
- Marketing (in some cases)
- Lifestyle Changes
- Impact on Those Around Us

This phase will take a lot of thinking. This is where you will need to dream about reaching your endeavor, and visualizing the implementation. You must really feel comfortable with this visualization. It is hard to succeed at something unless you can visualize it.

Note

Visualization has become a powerful tool in just about all aspects of life; from sports to music to business ventures. I remember when I was taking classical guitar lessons (as an adult), and I wanted to know the best way to practice and perform. I found it very odd that visualization was such an important part in both of these activities. The recent books I obtained on performing indicated that most professionals spend the majority of their time prior to a concert just visualizing themselves playing the selections they were going to perform.

> The concept was to visualize the music, staff, and notes; and to see themselves playing it. Much to my surprise, they did not spend last minute time actually practicing.

As part of the planning process it is best to just write down all tasks, events, needs and ideas randomly as a list. This is a good time to keep a pad and pencil with you to jot things down – a hand-held recorder is even a better idea. Many of our best ideas come when we are driving the car, or jogging or walking, etc. As you write these things down think them over. You may want to do a little research in books and on the internet, but it is not necessarily required. After all, one of your program tasks may become researching, and several tasks can be performed simultaneously once you get going. For now, just keep thinking. Don't place time constraints on your planning development. "Defining endeavors" and "Planning" are so important that you should not go to the next step until you feel comfortable that you have completed this planning.

> ☑ Don't say you don't have enough time. You have exactly the same number of hours per day that were given to Helen Keller, Louis Pasteur, Michelangelo, Mother Teresa, Leonardo de Vinci, Thomas Jefferson, and Albert Einstein .[1]

This visualization is something most of us have done all our lives. If you're a man you probably remember playing by yourself in the back yard – just you and a football. You threw a pass to yourself, and ran into the end zone (denoted by the Maple tree) – Touchdown! It wins the game in the final seconds! The crowd leaps to their feet with a thunderous applause! The television announcer talks about you as the

114

best quarterback ever (or receiver – whichever you are this time). The girls want to meet you as you walk from the stadium after the game. This was visualizing!

I remember when I used to run a few miles a day when I was a young adult (nice way of saying kid). If there was another runner ahead of me somewhere, I had to beat him. Again, in my mind I was now competing in the world Olympics. That runner ahead was the only competitor ahead of me, and he was the favored runner. He was last year's Gold Medallist (of course). Here I was the unknown closing in on him. The TV announcers were scrambling for information on who this unknown person (me) was that was closing in on the champion. Of course, I beat him (unbeknownst to the real life runner), and became the new Gold Medallist, and breaking the world record.

In sales one of the most important techniques they teach you is to get the potential customer to visualize using your product. For example, you are selling widgets, and you find out the customer can increase production considerably if they use your widgets. They are higher quality, and result in the production of less scrap pieces; increasing production efficiency. As you are talking to the client you say, "Joe, imagine next month's production report after using our Super Widget. The number of scrap pieces will be almost zero, and your production rate will increase by 10%; about 10,000 more parts per month. Just think what it will be like, Joe, at your monthly managers meeting when you tell everyone how your production line was responsible for the increase in overall production, and subsequent profits. You'll be a hero, Joe!"

By the same token, don't let the planning process go on forever – there will always be some changes going on with the plan no matter how well defined it becomes. This process of visualization, or dreaming, is very important. Do it!

If you can visualize it – you can make it happen!

A good way to start planning is to list the obstacles, and calculate the resources needed. Then, you need to buffer these projections so that you are very conservative in your projections. In other words, if you have conservatively determined that you will need $15,000 to reach your endeavor, then add 15% to this making it $17,250 (i.e. 15% times $15,000 = $2,250, and $2,250 + $15,000 = $17,250). Do the same thing with projecting time. If you determine, conservatively, that it will take 90 days (about 3 months) to overcome an obstacle, then buffer it by 15% or 104 days. I just randomly picked 15% because that is what I have used in business buffers. You can use whatever you want, 10%, 20%, etc.).

I realize we are talking in general terms, and have not defined what the obstacles are, etc, but the point is we always need to build in a little buffer for when we may have miscalculated, or for when something unexpected is incurred. If it turns out that we didn't need the buffer, great. It is always best to not come up short. Think of it as if you were submitting a pro forma to the bank to obtain a loan. You would always build as much conservatism into the plan as possible.

There are a whole myriad of barriers that can delay or slow down implementation. The idea is to first identify these barriers, and then figure out how to deal with them. You may be thinking, "This is where I started. I know what I want to do, but I just can't because there are too many other things in the way." Well, now is the time to organize your life so that these things aren't "barriers" but rather "obstacles" to overcome. Your plan will define how to overcome them. We'll come back to the "time" aspect later. We need to look at the "money" aspect for a few minutes. Also, don't forget that by reading how our mythical scenarios deal with implementation will help you.

Resources (Money)

The biggest barrier to reaching our dreams is usually the available recourses needed; specifically money. That's why most people see money as the answer to all their problems. In a way, it is because it provides the means to do what we want. The problem is when people don't really know what they want to do then the means just lets them bounce around life not feeling the fulfillment of doing what makes them happy (self-actualization?). We now know what we want; so now we can figure a way to get the means to do it.

Money is a funny thing. For most of us we live either at the top of our means or beyond it. No matter how much we make, we seem to use it all up "living." We can't seem to save very much. How many times have we tried to live on a budget that will save money for those unexpected situations (e.g. auto maintenance), but can't seem to? It is like losing weight – difficult! We have to reach down and find that lost human trait called "self-discipline." I know you don't want to hear someone tell you all this again. You know what you "*should do*," and you'll do it when you decide to! Right? Well, now is the time to "decide to." How many times have you said, "This is the first day of the rest of my life?" Hey, me too!

Let's see, how can I motivate you?

Think about this. Assuming you live in the United States, you are one of the fortunate people that have freedoms that the majority of people in the world don't have. Most don't have the resources or opportunity to do much more than live somewhere at the bottom two levels of Maslow's hierarchy of Needs (i.e. physiological and safety needs). Here in the U.S. we are living with the opportunity billions of other people would die to have (*Many people in our country have died for these freedoms and opportunities*). Are we maybe taking our life situation for granted? We almost owe it to the rest of the world and those that gave their lives to make the most of our fortunate predicament. Think about the hardship, helplessness and diminished hope so many people suffered during war times. And think how they appreciated peace and a place to rest their bodies. They lived through mental and physical anguish in order to live a free life. And they did it for their children and for us too. That's right! It's time to change our acceptance of our situation and go for it. When will we do it – Later? Then, all of a sudden we're 90 years old and wondering why we never did. Do you know what the problem is? It is that all of this takes some effort. We decide we're going to lose weight, or quit smoking, or quit drinking, or save money, or whatever. We start out with a plan, and then we are tired toward the end of the day. We sit down and watch television for relaxation and then need a snack or a beer or a cigarette. We know when we do it that it is a habit, but hey we messed up this time and, "We'll just start again tomorrow." No! If you're too tired to maintain a positive, productive

118

mindset – Go to Bed. Wake up fresh tomorrow and continue on – you won't have to start over! Don't slide back at the end of the day because when you wake up and remember you didn't give up and you stayed on the diet or continued not to smoke you will feel phenomenal! The same goes for your pursuance of a personal endeavor.

By the way, I don't have a problem with starting over each day. I mean, it is difficult to make life changes; so, we need to keep trying. But we will feel so much better if we can stay on our course and our plan. It is worth recalling that most of the very successful people failed over and over many times. Look at Abraham Lincoln, he had eleven (11) major life and career failures, and Maslow considered him as one of the few people he based his definition of reaching self-actualization on. Failure is when a set back or obstacle becomes a barrier. It is your mind that will make that definition. Remember the saying, "An overnight success takes about 15 years?"

Don't worry, I haven't forgotten that we're supposed to be talking about money as it relates to the implementation of our plan, but all of this is related. I need to make some statements about what I have learned in my life. When you write your book, you can do the same.

I have had to fight weight gain all my life. As a child I was definitely overweight, or politically, incorrectly fat. In fact, when I was an infant in the hospital they had to feed me twice as often, and they put little mittens on my hands, and tied them down because I kept trying to eat my hands.

119

Somewhere around the eighth grade I started losing weight because I was growing taller. When I entered high school I was actually about normal in weight because I had grown to a height of 6' 4", and I had worked during the summer at my aunt's farm, and was an avid basketball player. However, from then on it has been a lifetime effort to stay "not fat."

It was easier when I was in high school and college because at that age we all have higher metabolism rates, and are very active. My weight was around 210 lbs (just about right for my age and height). One summer I actually got down to 165 lbs from working two jobs in the summer during college. That was too skinny. Later in life I have gotten to as much as 250 lbs, but in the last several years I have been able to keep it down to close to my recommended weight. I have always lifted weights and jogged or run most of my life. I played a lot of sports, and like the feeling of "being in shape."

Why am I telling you all this? Because I want to establish some credibility with the struggles people have with addictions and difficult habits to break. For me, and I believe for a vast number of others, being healthy and feeling "in shape" makes me happier and more efficient in every other aspect of my life. For the majority of people I think body maintenance has been lost to a low place in life's priorities. When you're healthy and fit you feel like you are a clean, new car. You have more energy, and you are more attractive to yourself and others.

> **I feel, for me, health and fitness is "key" to my life. It is key to making me feel like pursuing my life plan, and it is key to helping me overcome the routine "downs" in life that we all experience.**

120

**If I am feeling down, and get out of the
shower and look in the mirror and feel
like I look good, it really helps me.**

In my personal implementation in reaching my endeavor
one of my sub objectives was to devise a way to get and stay
in shape as a permanent part of my life style. I feel it helps
to reinforce my self-discipline, and make me generally more
positive and open to pursuing my life endeavor.

Now, back to money. Saving money is similar to losing
weight and maintaining health. It needs to take a higher
priority. In money management books one of the first
things they say is you should make sure to "pay yourself
first." Well, you looked at defining your endeavors that are
self-centered to you. Now, it is time to find money and save
it; again for yourself.

Of course, you need to determine how much money you
require to proceed with your plan. For someone that wants
to open a restaurant it will be different than for someone
that wants to take piano lessons. We will talk about how to
determine what you need in terms of money; but first, there
are some ways listed in the following pages that you may
never have thought of to find or save money.

Of course, you can decide to save a portion of your income,
and this is an excellent idea, but there are ways to save
money by considering saving money that you would have
spent elsewhere but didn't. In other words, every time you
save money by not doing something you were going to do,
put that money away in a savings account anyway; as if you
had spent it. I am not talking about decisions not to spend
the money because you can't afford it. I'm talking about
those expenditures that you decided not to make for some
other reason, like deciding you really didn't need it at the

last moment. These kinds of expenditures would have been made, and you would never have missed the money because that's the way life is. So, if you wouldn't miss it anyway, why not put it into a savings account?

1. If you're a non-smoker, figure up how much you are saving by not smoking and once a month put that amount into the savings account. Let's say, for example, a pack of cigarettes costs $3.50. For a pack-a-day habit $3.50 times 365 days a year equals $1,278 per year; or $107 per month. Round it off and put $110 into the savings account each month.

2. If you're a non-drinker figure up what you're saving and put that into the savings account.

3. Are you a two family income? Have you based your lifestyle on both incomes? If so, try and wean yourself down to one income or at lease not the full two incomes. Whatever you can wean from your lifestyle put it into the savings account.

4. Do you have one or more cars that are paid for? If so, place whatever monthly payment you would be paying for one or more of the vehicles into the savings account. You know that some day again you will have to buy a new vehicle and you will find a way to make the monthly payment then; so, why not find a way now?

5. How about home maintenance insurance; do you have any? When I bought the house I am living in I bought a year's worth of home maintenance insurance. I tried to use it once to fix the garage door, but the small print of the insurance policy said it would pay for fixing the electronic garage door, all except the opener mechanism. Of course, that was the part I needed. So, when I received a letter to renew the policy for $399 a year, I declined and put that amount into the savings account. I make notes on all deposits I make to the savings account so I'll know where it came from. I also put it on the calendar to pay the same amount again next year to the savings account just as if I had decided to keep the insurance plan and make payments.

6. I did the same thing with a life insurance policy I had on myself. My wife and I decided that we didn't really need it anymore, and since it was a term plan it really had no cash value. It was about $1,500 per year. Now each year I put $1,500 into the savings account just like I still have the policy.

7. There are so many ways to save money when you think about it. Maybe you decided to start a remodeling project in or outside the house. Maybe you were seriously considering doing it, but something changed your mind; not lack of money – something else. You could put this money into the savings account since for all practical purposes you would have spent it

back then and never missed it now. I did this with a small project in the bathroom. I planned on installing a sliding shower door on the bath tub in a bathroom. I delayed doing it while I tried to condition the water so that there was less iron in it. I was never able to reduce the iron to a level that I thought it wouldn't stain the new sliding door. So, I never installed it, and decided we could live with just the shower curtain. I had calculated that it would have cost me about $450 to make the improvement; so, I put $450 into the savings account.

8. Did you ever go shopping and find some clothing or shoes that you were going to buy, and then right before you went to the check-out you decided not to buy one or more of the items? It wasn't the money; it was just that you didn't really need it right now. So, when you get home put whatever amount of money you were going to spend on the items into the savings account. Remember, you were going to spend it anyway.

9. How about when you buy some clothing and it turns out not to be quite the right size. You take it back, and they don't have the size you need. Do you buy the item at a later time? Probably not; so, why not put that returned money into the savings account?

10. Do you go out to eat much? I go out to eat with friends almost every Saturday. There

are those times when something comes up and I'm not able to do it. I calculate what I would have spent that night and deposit it into the savings account.

11. How about when you get bad service at a restaurant? I tip generously when I get good service, adequately when I get normal service, and less if I get poor service. If I get adequate or poor service I calculate the difference in tip I would have given for excellent service, and it goes into the savings account. If you save even a couple bucks, you can have a box to put it in at home until it is sufficient to make a savings deposit. Don't wait too long, though; you may spend it in a weak moment. It's harder to spend when it's in an account at the bank.

12. I collect all change from my pockets and any that is laying around in the car and house. Each day I change clothes I put the change in the large plastic cup in my bedroom. I've become good at finding change lying around; especially on the washer and dryer. When the cup is full I take it to the grocery store where they have those machines that take it and count it and give you a receipt for cash. I get the cash and put it into the savings account.

13. How about when someone invites you over to dinner? Figure up what you are saving on food and put it into the savings account.

14. Did you get a raise at work? Can you still live on what you were making prior to the raise? If so, put the difference into the savings account.

15. Have a garage sale and put the profit into the savings account.

16. Sell some items you have been meaning to get rid of (e.g. bicycles, TVs, musical instruments, etc.).

17. You were going to buy a new riding lawnmower, but decided it was just too expensive. Hey, you can get by with the old one. How about putting about half of what you would have paid for a new one in the savings account? You would have spent about half if you could have found a mower for that price anyway.

18. Did you get money for your birthday or Christmas? You know where to put it.

19. Did you get a gift that is something you would never buy or wear? Yep, take it back and get the cash. It's not that you don't appreciate the gift and the thought, but this is a much better gift.

20. One time I took my old van to the dealership because the air conditioner wasn't working. They said I needed a new compressor, Freon, etc. - to the tune of about $350. That seemed like a lot to spend on such an old vehicle. I took it to a private mechanic

that I had trusted for years. I didn't tell him what the dealership had told me, but he looked it over and just put Freon in for $30 (this was before Freon was determined to be a contributor dissolving the ozone layer – that's another story – don't get me started). So, if I had used the dealership I would have spent over $320 more. Maybe you are thinking that you never would have been so stupid as to pay the dealership quote anyway, but hey why not reward yourself for being smart? You know many others would have just paid the dealership and not been as smart. Put the $320 in the savings account.

21. Do you go to a grocery store that has a customer card that provides savings to many items? I do, and when they ring up the sale they hand me the receipt, and tell me how much I have saved using the card. Guess what? I've started putting that savings into the bank. Yes, I know that the price is hiked up so the card use allows "normal" cost, but, Hey! – so what.

22. I take medicine on a routine basis, and the prescription cost has been becoming significant. Recently, I found a prescription store in my neighborhood that sold drugs via a Canadian connection. The cost for some drugs was at an 80% discount. So, now I put the difference I am saving into the account.

See how this works? Once you begin looking for reasons to account for savings or unspent money it becomes a challenge, even a game. Make it as easy as possible to do this. I have on-line banking, and so I just transfer the money from my checking account to the savings account over the computer. I don't have to physically take cash to the bank and deposit it for each time I make one of these savings.

I found that it is important to document these deposits (transfers) for a couple of reasons. One, if it is something like a policy payment that I would have made annually or semiannually I want to know when to make that deposit the next year. Also, it serves as a reminder of what all I have done, so I will continue to make these deposits. It's another way of confirming how you are doing in saving money and accomplishing something worthwhile. I just made an entry into my computer using word processing program. I enter the date, then a description of what the deposit was. If you want to use a spreadsheet, and take it a step further, that's up to you. You'll see an actual example of this accounting in one of the upcoming scenarios.

I realize that it sounds sort of obsessive-retentive to do all this nit-picking savings. You probably think I'm some sort of savings nut. Actually, I tend to be just the other way. I am sort of a "happy-go-lucky" person that doesn't mind spending money. I'm not the real worrying type; so, this is what works well for me. It allows me to save money by rationalizing that I would have spent it anyway.

Once endeavors have been defined and some planning considered it will be time to implement the way in which we are going to achieve these endeavors. We can't really just blindly follow a plan without seeing the light at the end of the tunnel. Implementation will consist of Planning, Monitoring

& Measurement and Review. During the planning phase we will define accurately the tasks we will need to complete to reach our endeavor. Then, in the Monitoring/Measurement stage we will define the order in which events will occur (tasks will be completed), and we will set up a chart to allow us to view how we are doing as time goes by. Finally, we will set up a frequency to review how things are going. This will allow us to make adjustments, modifications and analyze the process.

Don't forget that this process is a program, not a project. Each part of the implementation process will be on-going. We will constantly be looking at what we are doing so we can change with the times, incorporate new ideas, re-evaluate our direction and confirm our desires.

Chapter 11 – Time & Monitoring/Measurement

Once you feel comfortable with all the tasks you will have to complete to reach your endeavor it is time to set them down as chronological events. To do this you must prioritize all your random noted tasks. List them in order of which should be started first. Some tasks will be completed in a short time, and others may be ongoing throughout the entire program (and the rest of your life). Many of the tasks may be completed at the same time (in parallel), and others may not be able to be started until another task is completed first (consecutively).

Once the list is prioritized, then you can start to estimate how long each individual task will take. With this information you can then create a timeline chart that depicts when each task begins and ends, and the overlap of tasks in parallel. The chart date will start when you decide to begin the first task. The ending chart date will be the date that the last task ends. These tasks are now called events.

Of course, this is a program and not a project; so, in actuality there is no end point to the chart. However, creating such an endless chart would take the same amount of time as calculating infinity. So, pick a point at which the majority of implementation is completed, and operation or maintenance of your endeavor starts. When you get close to the end of that chart you can create another chart for the next, on-going phase of the program. You will see an example of how this chronology and time chart is done in the upcoming scenario of Sam Single.

Chapter 12 - Continual Review

This final part of the process is just as important as all other parts; however, people will tend to slack off in completing it. You must define a review frequency in order to thoroughly evaluate how the program is going. This frequency will be different for different people and for different endeavors. In fact, you may wish the review frequency to change within the process. For example, you may need to review things more frequently at first, and then less frequently as change becomes less frequent during implementation. Regardless of what changes are occurring you should never review less frequently than twice a year; even when implementation is complete.

So what do you do in the review? You do a structured evaluation of what has happened since the last review. You can only do this, of course, if you write down the minutes of the previous review. Yes, it is mandatory that you write down notes (minutes) of your review in detail, and then file them away in a safe place. As an example, each review could be stored in a separate manila file folder and placed in a hanging file.

This review is going to allow you to continually improve upon your endeavor, and continually help you find your shortcomings (of course if you're like me you don't have any – humor). It should be taken seriously, and you should take your time to make sure it is complete. You may decide to write it up as minutes, or preferably as a detailed report with timeline charts and maybe graphs indicating success or departures from the "projected." How detailed you become is dependent upon what you like to do. This review process is also another way of keeping your mind focused on your endeavor. Remember, "Out of sight – out of mind."

You should also have a written protocol or agenda for the review. You should make it as detailed as you can. It will be different for each person, but some main agenda topics should be included in everyone's review:

1. General Overview Comments
   Old Business
   New Business

2. Budget Review
   Old Business
   New Business

3. Timeline Review
   Old Business
   New Business

4. Individual Event
   Review
   Old Business
   New Business

5. Problems and Corrections
   Old Business
   New Business

6. New Events
   Old Business
   New Business

7. Miscellaneous
   Old Business
   New Business

Each review topic should include a subsection of "Old Business" and "New Business" so that continuity can exist between current and previous review meetings.

Let's look at how the scenario people deal with this implementation. It will give you some ideas to use.

Chapter 13 – Sam's Implementation

Planning - Step 1 (Implementation)

If you recall, Sam has decided his endeavor is to own a restaurant where he cannot only enjoy the skills he has developed from previous jobs, but also to have his own place to perform his music. He will get to interface with people routinely (which he really enjoys), and he will get to have other musical guests perform also.

The first thing he needs to do is sit down and do some dreaming and thinking. He needs to visualize what he wants to happen. He should think about what atmosphere and ambiance he wants the restaurant to have. Will it be a smaller café' style place or would it best be in a new building or in an older home with some classic character? He should think about what the menu will consist of, and how many people he will need to help operate the establishment. Another thing for him to consider is the possibility of starting small and expanding in phases. Sam needs to do a lot of thinking like this and taking notes of his thoughts.

His next step will be to research restaurants, café's, coffee shops, etc., but first he needs to do all the dreaming and thinking on his own. Why? People can have their own ideas on how things should be, but if they are influenced by what is considered "standard practices," then these original or unique ideas may never be considered. In so many cases, the popularity or success of a business venture lies in what sets it apart from other such ventures. The uniqueness is something that many times comes from within people who think about things differently. So, Sam and everyone else should always develop their own ideas and dreams first before being influenced by the rest of the world.

Note

It is always a good idea to make sure that whatever endeavor one embarks upon that they become familiar with the standard practices of that endeavor. It avoids making unneeded mistakes and definitely eliminates a big portion of the learning curve. Why reinvent the wheel? Having said this, there have been many cases where people did things their own way and became successful because of it. Take Seabiscuit the racehorse. He was too small to be a racehorse. Also, take music as another example. Some of the greatest recent composers of popular music created songs that had a different sound. Why? Because they didn't really listen to that much music, and subsequently they were not influenced by "accepted" musical progressions and styles.

As a guitar player I am reminded of Tommy Tedesco, one of the best guitarists ever. When I first heard some of his music on the radio I thought, "That's just what I want to be, a classical guitarist that can use that style to add interest in playing jazz on the guitar." Upon further investigation it turned out Tommy was at the top of heap when it comes to studio musicians. That is, he is a musician's musician. His accomplishments included innumerable movie and television musical credits. To hear him play is to hear the most beautiful classical guitar sound. Guess what? He never had a classical guitar lesson, and doesn't play classical. Tommy looks like a bus driver (as he describes himself). He has stubby, thick little fingers and plays using a combination of pick style and finger style methods (something he developed on his own). He plays a classical guitar, but holds it all wrong, and fingers it incorrectly. He is the epitome of incorrectness. The guitar teacher would tell you that he could never become any good with such unacceptable fundamentals. Hey, don't tell Tommy, ok?

It is important to understand, however, that one must always research the area of their endeavor, regardless. There are laws and rules that we need to be aware of. There are ways of doing things that have come out of years of experience. So, I am not suggesting that Sam should just follow his dreams, only. I am saying Sam should make sure he has dreamed his own way before he is exposed to the standards of the world. Sam did this. Here's what he came up with.

Business Concept

Ultimately, the establishment will be a full time restaurant; serving a full menu of selections. The size will never be large, and the menu will consist of American, home style cooking. It is preferred that the building be an older house converted into a restaurant. It is felt that it should be geared to the "baby boomer" age group. Sam was thinking that the "over 45" age group would be people that would best enjoy a relaxing atmosphere, and be ready to listen to music and to enjoy a low key environment. He figured the young adult age group (early twenties) would either be single (and not interested), or married, but on a budget that would not favor his place. Besides, Sam didn't envision his place as a family restaurant with lots of kids. It was, after all, going to be a place to enjoy live music as well as a relaxed dining atmosphere.

The converted older home would add character to the place, and the inside would seem homey, but yet decorated with very upscale aesthetic interior design. The location, also, would be very important. It needed to be out in the suburbs where the baby boomers lived, but yet in an area that had older homes; possibly a historically renovated area.

Of course, Sam realized that all these requirements may be difficult to meet; so, he convinced himself to have flexible expectations. If all his requirements couldn't be met he would settle for less, with the acknowledgement that he could always upgrade or change aspects as they presented themselves down the road. Finally, he decided it may be best to implement his endeavor in phases.

Phase I

Sam decided it would be best to start off slow; especially since he had never owned a restaurant before. He thought perhaps he would concentrate on finding a house first. By the way, he never planned on quitting his day job until the new venture could pay for itself. He thought he could buy the house and live in it while he prepared for the initial part of his plan.

The initial part of his plan was to offer a dinner once or twice a month. This dinner would be by reservation only, and would be limited to just a couple of full dinner menu selections. Sam had gotten this idea from some other such restaurants around the area. In fact, many of them offered these dinners with a theme (e.g. holidays and anniversaries). This would allow him to get accustomed to providing the services while he had time to learn. He even considered opening it up to a Bed & Breakfast during the initial phase. This could also allow a degree of learning. There were all kinds of advantages to starting off slow like this. He could have a place to live, to practice music, and he could still renovate and decorate at leisure.

Phase II

The next phase would consist of expanding the hours of operation. Not only would he still offer the monthly or bimonthly dinners, but he would also expand it into a café style place with limited hours during lunch on Thursday and Friday, and Open on Friday and Saturday evenings. The food would consist of sandwiches and salads; perhaps on bagels or unique breads. The emphasis would be on freshness, and taste. Coffee and soft drinks would be the beverages, and Friday and Saturday nights would offer live music. This would allow him to phase the activities of finding musical entertainment.

Phase III

This would be the final and full-scale restaurant. It would still offer live music, and would now be open full time with an expanded menu.

With this concept in mind, it was time for Sam to learn more about the restaurant business, as well as about running a business in general. He went to the library and bookstore and found a myriad of books on both topics. He also found some very helpful information on the Internet. He selected several books that he felt would be best to start with. Although he was good at service and entertainment, he was weak in the area of legal aspects such as permits and health considerations concerned with the food industry. He also needed to know things like which form of business structure would be best for him (e.g. sole proprietorship, or partnership, or incorporation, etc.). He also needed to know ways in which to raise money for business ventures. He didn't know what route he would take in terms of financial support (if any), but he wanted to know all the options.

We could almost call what Sam is doing is writing a business plan. It really isn't one yet because it is broader than a business plan; however, it will help him immensely if he does need to write a business plan. He may not realize it at this point, but he will eventually research a lot about the business he is going into before it is all over, but he will be wiser for it, and will have a better chance of succeeding the first time. The reason I say "the first time" is because many people fail over and over again in the pursuit of their dreams. Since they are determined they eventually make it, but by doing a little research first this can, many times, be avoided.

By the way, during all this planning portion of the implementation, Sam has already begun to save money, by incorporating some of the ideas we discussed previously. For example, Sam is both a smoker and drinker to some degree. He wasn't an alcoholic or anything, but living a life of an alternative rock guitarist, for at least part of his life, he did put away about three six-packs of beer a week, and a pack of cigarettes a day. He couldn't just quit "cold turkey," but he did feel he could significantly cut back. Here's the way he figured it:

- One pack a day of cigarettes = $3.50 per day or $3.50 times 365 days = $1,278 per year. If he cut back to ½ a pack it would be a savings of $639 per year (or approximately $53 per month.

- Three six-packs of beer a week = $15 a week or $15 times 52 weeks per year = $780 per year. If he cut it back to 1 six-pack per week he would save $520 per year (or $43 per month).

So, he put $96 (savings on beer and cigarettes) into the savings account each month. This would amount to a savings of $1,152 per year. He also knew if he eventually quit smoking and drinking, altogether, he would be able to save a total of $2,058 per year. Just think, in five years he could save $10,290 just from cigarettes and beer.

Sam also did a little more calculating. He determined that he went out drinking and eating three times a week; Wednesdays, Fridays and Saturdays. He also mostly ate fast food the other days of the week because he was single, after all. He did the Wednesday, Friday and Saturday night thing to basically meet women and socialize with his buddies. He thought about how he was going to devote more time to reaching his endeavor. He wasn't that crazy about the Wednesday and Saturday nights out. First, getting to work the next morning after Wednesday night out was a hassle, especially for the benefit he was getting from it. He felt like if it wasn't that his buddies kept wanting him to go out with them that he, himself, probably wouldn't go out. As far as Saturday nights go, it was mostly the "date night" crowd, and he wasn't dating anyone currently. So, he could do without that night out too.

If he did eliminate some of this social time, would he get lonely? He thought about it, and he remembered how lucky he is to live in the great country of America, and decided he would do these cutbacks. Perhaps he could visit his parents and grandparents more. Maybe he will meet new people as he pursues his endeavor; maybe people in the restaurant business.

He decided he would go out just once a week on Fridays. He calculated what he typically spent in food and beer on these nights out. He would eat a bigger dinner than normal and then go to a singles type bar with the guys until about 1:00 or 2:00 am, and then they would either stop at a fast food place or go have breakfast somewhere. He figured he paid about $12 for dinner, then $35 for beer during the evening, and sometimes a cover charge of $3. Then, on the way home he would spend, on the average, about $6 in fast food. He wondered how much gas he was saving by not going out two days a week, but decided it was negligible. So this totaled $56 a night (or $168 a week for the three nights). That did seem about right.

Actually, he thought it was maybe a little conservative. Maybe he spent more on drinks, come to think of it. He did do shots and liquor from time to time. Also, he did play some darts and games that cost money at the bars too. Ok, for now he decided to stay conservative and use the original estimates. If he did cut out the Wednesdays and Saturdays he would save $112 a week (or $485 a month or $5,820 a year).

This was getting very interesting. So now what was he saving by doing these two changes? Well, about ($5,820/yr divided by 12 mo/yr = $485) + ($96/mo in cigarettes and beer) = $581 total per month, or $6,972 per year. Could he really be spending that much a year on these non-essentials? That would be $34,860 saved in five years, and $69,720 saved in ten years. Heck, he could put down a 20% payment on a conventional mortgage for his café/restaurant with this savings. He was really starting to be amazed at what he could potentially save.

He was due to get a $1 an hour raise at work. What if he could just save that increase too; what would it amount to? He estimated that 40 hours a week times 52 weeks equaled 2080 hours, or $2,080 (at $1 per hour), or $10,400 in five years or $20,800 in ten years. So altogether (including the beer and cigarette savings) he could save $45,260 in five years and $90,520 in ten years. Hey? He was averaging a $1 raise every two years; what savings would that result in? Let's see?

Now, at this point you may be saying to yourself, "Come on Ron, I get the point – how far are you going to take this?" Well, I don't mean to insult your intelligence (I know this isn't rocket science mathematics), and I don't want to bore you, but it is about over. I won't be going into any such detail in any of the other scenario people discussions. Think of it as your own money. Once you do that then it becomes a little more interesting.

We already calculated $2,080 for the first year. Since the next raise would not be for two years, the second year savings would also be $2,080; totaling $4,160 after two years. In the third and fourth years he would have an additional $1 increase; so, years three and four would result in a savings of $4,160 per year (or $8,320 for the total of years three and four).

So, up through year four the savings is now $12,480. The fifth year would be another $1 increase resulting in a savings of $6,240 just for that year. After five years the savings would be $18,729 (just from pay increases). Total savings including the other areas of savings would be $53,583 in five years. If we continued the $1 raise every two years through to ten years the savings from pay increases would be $62,409 or total of $132,129 after ten years. Wow!!

Hey? What if he put the money in a Certificate of Deposit at 3% interest; what additional money would he make? Well, about $1,607 more on $53,583 and about $3,964 on

$132,129. What about if he invested it into some mutual funds yielding an average return on investment (ROI) of 8%? That would be $4,287 on $53,583 and $10,570 on $132,129. Don't you just love math when it involves making money? Sam started looking everywhere he could to rationalize depositing as much money into the savings account as possible.

Monitor/Measure – *Step 2 (Implementation)*

While Sam was reading up on restaurant operation, as well as ways to get capital, he also needed to project (estimate) just how long it would take to implement his endeavor, and what information he would look at to help keep him on course. This is the part of implementation that is referred to as *monitoring and measurement*.

For now, perhaps he doesn't know all the information he will need to calculate accurate needs, but at least he can do some estimating to get started. One way to do this is to estimate when he thought he would be able to complete certain tasks toward obtaining his endeavor.

He first needed to just jot down everything he could think of that needed to be done, and estimate how much time each item would take. For the sake of brevity we will list just some of the major items. I'm sure Sam could get even more detailed by listing additional items that fall under each of these categories.

Notes Listed Randomly

Tasks	Time Required
- Acquire/save about $80,000	- 3 years
- Buy/rent/lease place of business	- 1 year
- Read up on business (regs, operation, etc.)	- 6 months
- Write Business Plan	- 2 months
- Remodel/decorate	- 8 months
- Hire help	- 1 month
- Market research	- 2 months
- Research/observe competition	- 3 months
- Line up entertainment	- 3 months
- Design advertising	- 1 month
- Purchase equipment (food preparation)	- 2 months
- Purchase furniture, tables, chairs, etc.	- 3 months
- Determine menu	- 2 months
- Test run	- 1 month
- Personal health and fitness program	- on-going

Sam needed to rearrange these in order of chronology, or in order of what needs to be done first to last.

Notes Listed in Consecutive Order

Tasks	Time Required
- Acquire/save about $80,000	- 3 years
- Personal health and fitness program	- on-going
- Read up on business (regs, operation, etc.)	- 1 year
- Conduct market research	- 2 months
- Research/observe competition	- 3 months
- Write Business Plan	- 2 months
- Buy/rent/lease place of business	- 1 year
- Remodel/decorate	- 8 months
- Purchase furniture, tables, chairs, etc.	- 3 months
- Purchase Equipment	- 2 months
- Determine menu	- 2 months
- Design advertising	- 1 month
- Line up entertainment	- 3 months
- Hire help	- 1 month
- Test run	- 1 month

Ok, now he was getting a better handle on things. He could use this list as is, but charting such information provides a better visualization of how things will progress. In the next figure you can see one way in which Sam could chart this chronology of events. Such charts almost always provide a time line across the bottom (horizontally) with events to be accomplished represented by bars.

In the chart there are two series of bars. One bar is for what Sam estimates to happen (projected). The other bar is what actually occurs (actual), and will be updated as time goes by. The vertical line, on this example, just indicates the current day so that you can see how the "actual" compares to the "projected" up through the current day.

This type of chart will allow a quick visualization of how Sam is "meeting" his defined tasks toward reaching his endeavor. Of course, the estimated portion may change as he becomes more knowledgeable about the expectations. A chart like this can be created on the computer using many of the popular spreadsheets and word processing programs. So, if you are the computer type it is an easy way to not only create such a chart, but to modify it as time goes by.

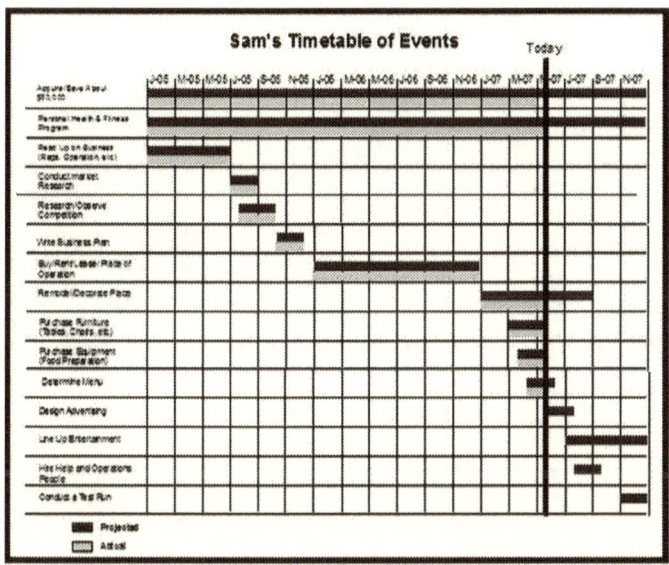

Chart Created Using Computer Software

If you are not the computer type person, don't worry. These timeline type charts were created many years before anyone used personal computers. By using a pencil and ruler you can make a very effective chart tool. See the next figure.

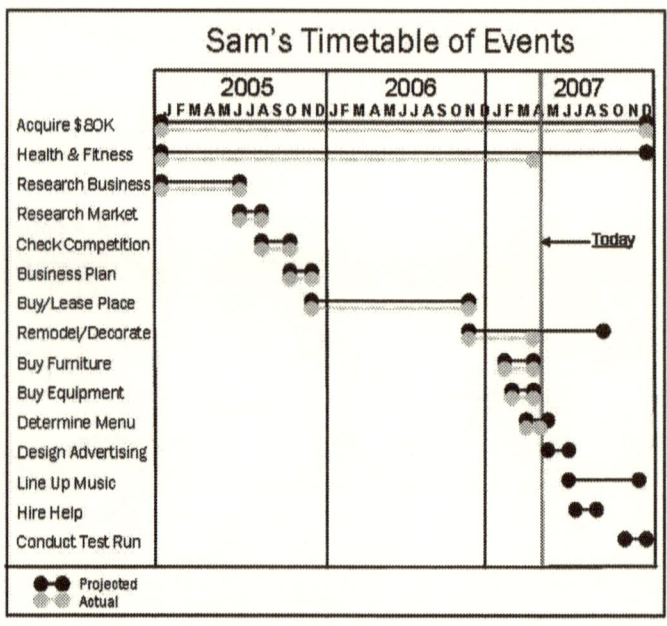

Chart Created with Pencil and Ruler

Continuous Review – *Step 3 (Implementation)*

Even though Sam has defined his expectations, and charted them for view, he still needs to review his program on a continuous basis. During this review he needs to actually write a review report to document what he has observed and any decisions he has made as a result.

Sam set up the review schedule for every three months for a couple of reasons. First, according to his time line chart several activities were scheduled to initiate and complete within three-month periods. Secondly, he felt with all the reading up on the restaurant business he was planning that he may learn some things that could cause him to make some adjustments in his plan. Remember, this initial planning and monitoring is only estimated from what knowledge he has currently.

Chapter 14 – Howard's Implementation

If you remember, Howard is in his late forties, and has a great family. He has a good job (self-employed), and from all outward appearances he looks successful and secure. In reality he has inadequate money for retirement, and feels like he is just "living to work." He wants to get more out of life. He suddenly realizes he has been living the American Dream of a big house, a family and all the extracurricular activities to go along with it. He has had a revelation that the American Dream is not "his" dream.

He determined that he was actually most interested in trading stocks on-line. He gained great satisfaction in learning about companies and the process of trying to project which stocks would go up and which would go down. It was time for him to implement his endeavor.

Planning - Step 1 (Implementation)

Business Concept

Ultimately, Howard wanted to be able to retire as early as possible. He wanted to make enough money in his retirement account to be able to live comfortably the rest of his life. The stock trading idea could make this happen. The exciting part is that he would also keep making money with a minimal amount of time and effort spent trading stocks even when he is retired (he sure is optimistic, isn't he? – ha!).

He needed to work out a schedule for when he would be able to be on-line to trade stocks. He needed to figure out a schedule to learn the stock trading business (on-going). He needed to project how much money he would be able to make over time, and how this would all fit into his current lifestyle and family needs.

One big difference between Howard and Sam Single is the fact that Howard is married, and he wants his wife to be intimately involved in his dream. It is critical that she be in agreement with his plans; so, before going any further he sat down with his wife and discussed the matter. She was excited that he had some direction in his life, but at the same time was not convinced about the exact opportunity.

Remember, he has been thinking and dreaming and doing self-introspection for a while; she is just learning about this revelation. Howard assures her that he will take the time to explain what he has been thinking, and even suggests that perhaps they could review some books on the subject; books both about trading as well as books about successes. Motivation by success stories is always helpful.

One of the things Howard has always recognized in himself is the effect of "feeling healthy" and "being in good shape" has had on his overall confidence and self-motivation. Like so many other people, however, he has not given his body the attention it needs for proper maintenance. He is about twenty pounds overweight, and has not done any routine exercise for a while. He knew he would have a much better chance at success with his plan if he got, and stayed, in shape. So, he decided his health and fitness was going to take a priority in his life. He also knew that weight control had been a struggle all of his life. Not so different from many of us, he had tried all kinds of diets from fasting to liquid diets.

Note

I want to re-emphasize a point here. Like everything else we do in life we must make a "conscious effort" for it to be successful. The saying: "Out of Sight, Out of Mind" is very true. We cannot count on our memory to keep us focused on everything we need to be focused on. Visual observation and reminders work very well. In terms of weight loss, it is also very important to "track" what we are doing. People say "I don't need to keep track of my caloric intake, I'll remember." If you have ever been successful at losing weight, however, you know that you must write down what you eat. People will spend hours exercising, and rationalizing why they can't lose weight (e.g. wrong types of foods, wrong combinations of foods, etc.) when in fact weight loss is simple – "Less calories in = weight loss" It is simply a mass balance equation.

Well, guess what? Howard is thinking just like me, imagine that! He decided that he would aim for a weight loss program of losing one pound per week, and he would make up a calorie-counting sheet and weigh himself each day and graph the weight data so he could see how he was doing. He would start this immediately, before he even went any further with the implementation of his plan.

Another thing he decided he would start immediately was a program to start accumulating money. Like Sam, he hadn't figured out how much he would need, but he wanted to at least start saving money now. He and his wife sat down and wrote down all the ideas they could come up with. They reviewed the list in this book, and added some of their own. They decided they would start out conservatively and just do a few of the ideas. Here was their plan:

1. **Wife's Life Insurance** – Howard's wife had a life insurance plan for $150,000. It was costing them $370 a year. The fact of the matter was that although she liked having this plan for her husband (it made her feel good), it was not needed. They definitely needed his life insurance plan for her, but not hers for him; so, they dropped hers, but put the premium amount into their savings account annually.

2. **Whole House Insurance** – They were still paying an annual premium for insurance on appliances and house-related items from when they had bought the house; not to be confused with "Home Owner's Insurance." They had never needed it, and they had always considered discontinuing it. They put this annual premium into the savings account also.

3. **Gym Membership** – They had a family membership to the local health club; however, no one but Howard had used it in the last two years. The kids were older, and his wife never had used it. They could save $300 a year if they converted it to a single membership.

4. **Beer, Wine and Cigarettes** – Howard and his wife did not smoke, and they really didn't drink liquor products that much; mainly when they were dining out with friends. They decided that they would credit themselves for not partaking in such habits.

5. **Magazine Subscriptions** - Howard also determined that there were a couple of magazine subscriptions that they really never used; so, he decided not to renew them, and put the money in the savings account.

6. **Auto Monthly Payment** – Two of the three vehicles that Howard and his wife owned were paid off; so, he remembered a time when he was actually making three monthly loan payments for vehicles. Funny how the elimination of those payments hasn't seemed to make much of a difference in additional money available now. He decided that he would at least pretend that he still had one of the payments, and would credit it to the savings account. Maybe he would add the other vehicle credit later.

7. **Loose Change** – Howard always threw his loose change into a large tin can, and when it was full he would take it to the local grocery store where he would run it through one of those coin machines. It always amounted to around $30 to $50 every two or three months. Now, he decided he would credit this money to the monthly account.

8. **Grocery Savings Card** – They purchased their groceries at the local store, which had a savings card. This card was scanned into the cash register each time items were purchased, and the savings on special items purchased was printed out on the receipt.

9. **Non-Purchased Savings** – Howard and his wife kind of liked the idea of crediting themselves for making money-saving decisions when they shopped. In other words, when they planned to buy something such as clothing, but at the

last minute decided they really didn't need it. Or maybe at the last minute they decided to buy the less expensive version of the item; then, they could credit the savings difference between the two items.

10. **Garage Sale** – Now seemed to be a good time to sell some things they had accumulated, and were just too busy to sell. They decided to ask the kids to run the garage sale. The kids could set it up, run it and then cleanup afterwards. For their efforts they were allowed to keep 50% of the profit.

11. **Sale of Special Items** – Howard had several items that he had been wanting to sell through the paper, but just hadn't made the time to do it. For example, he had an amplifier and speakers that he no longer used.

There were more ways to accumulate money, but Howard and his wife decided this would be a good start. Howard made up a Savings Sheet to keep track of all these savings and to act as a reminder on what to deposit. He decided that all the annual deposits (such as life insurance policy and health club membership dues) would be made at the end of just one or two months a year. Of course, if there became a significant number of these annual deposits he would probably want to spread the payments throughout the year so as to not cause a cash flow problem in one month. These annual deductions he listed separately as "Annual Deposits."

He also decided that there were certain credits (such as auto payments, magazine subscriptions, etc.) that were the same each month. These he listed separately as "Monthly Deposits."

For everything else, he listed separately by date, but only made the total cash deposit of each at the end of the month; like paying a bill. In this way, there wouldn't be a lot of little deposits made throughout the month. His list was typed in the computer, and once the deposits were actually made he made the color of the type black. As he was listing the monthly items (before they were deposited at the end of the month) he kept the color red. In this way, he knew just by looking at the sheet which items had been deposited, and which had not.

The following is the sheet Howard came up with. This sheet provided all the totals for deposits made, and allowed him to see what kind of savings he was accumulating.

Savings Sheet

Annual		Deposit in August of Each Year
$1,120	Total	
	$350	Elimination of Wife's Life Insurance
	$450	Elimination of House Maint. Insurance
	$300	Reduction in Gym Membership

Monthly		Deposit Each Month
$406	Total	
	$ 50	Credit for Non-Purchase of Beer/Wine
	$ 40	Credit for Non-Purchase of Cigarettes
	$ 21	Elimination of Unread Magazines
	$295	Credit for Auto Monthly Payment

Deposits		Individual Items Deposited Monthly
$961	Total-June	
6/3	$406	Monthly Deposits fro Above
6/5	$ 40	Coins
6/12	$ 49	Grocery Card
6/14	$ 1	Grocery Card
6/15	$ 9	Grocery Card
6/21	$ 15	Grocery Card
6/23	$ 13	Grocery Card
6/24	$ 79	Spent $49 on grill instead of $119

$762	Total-July	
7/1	$406	Monthly Deposits from Above
7/1	$ 32	Grocery Card
7/2	$ 2	Grocery Card
7/6	$ 21	Grocery Card
7/12	$ 11	Grocery Card
7/15	$ 2	Grocery Card
7/16	$ 3	Grocery Card
7/26	$ 70	Grocery Card
7/30	$215	Garage Sale

$1,346	Total-August	
8/1	$ 905	Annual Deposits from Above
8/1	$406	Monthly Deposits from Above
8/3	$ 14	Grocery Card
8/6	$ 21	Grocery Card

August data is gray in this figure, but would be red if this were in color.

After two months of tracking this information Howard was able to make some general estimates on what he would save per year. He had accumulated two full months of expense data (June and July). The total for each respectively was $961 and $762. However, to be conservative Howard subtracted out a couple of items from each month because they were not reflective of reoccurring savings from month to month. He took out the sale of the speakers and amplifier $349 (in June) and the garage sale $215 (in July). He left the savings from the grill (June) and the shoes and shorts (July) in because he figured over the year that this may not be far off from what would be an actual average.

So, after deducting these items the amounts changed to $612 in June ($961 - $349 = $612) and $547 in July ($762 - $215 = $547). Now, he averaged these two monthly numbers (($612 + $547)/2 months) and got $580 per month. This amounted to approximately $8,080 per year (i.e. $580 X 12 months = $6,960 + $1,120 (additional "annual savings") = $8,080). Not a bad start.

As you may remember, Howard is a small business owner. Even though he has no employees he does have the responsibilities as such. One of the benefits of owning a business is that he can control his own retirement account/s. There are a variety of structured accounts very similar to 401Ks (e.g. Keoghs, SEPs, etc.). He had a SEP. A SEP is a simplified method of retirement management. Basically, it allows the business owner to deposit a certain percentage of their business income into a retirement account and not pay taxes on it until it is withdrawn later in life. For example, if 15% of the business income may be deposited; then income of $100,000 per year will allow the deposit of $15,000 into the retirement account (actually, I believe the current percentage is 20%, but we'll use 15% in this scenario).

Of course, in retirement accounts the money cannot be withdrawn until the person retires, and as I said it is also not taxed until it is withdrawn. This is a significant advantage for stock trading. In non-retirement accounts all money made during the year is taxed at the end of the year, and typically at a high rate. As mentioned before, the more money one has to invest, the quicker money is made. The retirement account allows all money to accumulate without reduction by taxes.

Howard's concept was to first keep working because the only way to get "seed" money into the retirement account was from business income. Next, he would transfer all of the money he had in the insurance mutual fund (close it out) into his on-line SEP account. And the money he saved via the methods described above would be saved and act as a "backup" to the retirement account.

Howard had $125,000 in his retirement account. He did a little research and discovered that most mutual funds can return at least a 6% rate over ten or more years. He really felt that he could return a lot more than this rate by trading his own stocks. He was interested in determining what rate of return (ROI) he would need to make a million dollars in seventeen years. He would be 65 years old in seventeen years, and would like to retire at least by then. He started to do a little calculation on paper. He started by calculating what he would make after year one if he were to return 6%. He would start with the $125,000 he had currently, add $17,000 that he would add each year as the maximum annual SEP contribution based on his income. He would calculate the ROI just annually, and not include the $17,000 until after the 6% calculation. This would be the most conservative conditions.

157

$125,000 X 0.06 (6%) = \$7,500 + \$125,000 + \$17,000 = \underline{\$149,500}$

Then, he calculated the next year:

$149,500 X 0.06 = \$8,970 + \$149,500 + \$17,000 = \underline{\$175,470}$

Now, Howard decided to put this into a computer spreadsheet so that he could quickly calculate each seventeen years at varying ROI percentages. If you are not computer literate, then you would need to do it the old fashion way; as done above.

Here is Howard's simple spreadsheet. Notice the highlighted cell which has the formula displayed in the cell contents display area directly above the spreadsheet.

Microsoft Excel - Howards Stock						
File Edit View Insert Format Tools Data Window Help						
B4		=B3*0.06 +B3+17000				
	A	B	C	D	E	F	G
1	Year	Projection At 6%	Projection At 8%	Projection At 10%	Projection At 12%	Projection At 14%	Projection At 16%
2							
3	Start	$125,000	$125,000	$125,000	$125,000	$125,000	$125,000
4	Year 1	$149,500	$152,000	$154,500	$157,000	$159,500	$162,000
5	Year 2	$175,470	$181,160	$186,950	$192,840	$198,830	$204,920
6	Year 3	$202,998	$212,653	$222,645	$232,981	$243,666	$254,707
7	Year 4	$232,178	$246,665	$261,910	$277,938	$294,779	$312,460
8	Year 5	$263,109	$283,398	$305,100	$328,291	$363,049	$379,454
9	Year 6	$295,895	$323,070	$352,610	$384,686	$419,475	$457,167
10	Year 7	$330,649	$365,916	$404,872	$447,848	$495,202	$547,313
11	Year 8	$367,488	$412,189	$462,359	$518,590	$581,530	$651,883
12	Year 9	$406,537	$462,164	$525,595	$597,821	$679,944	$773,185
13	Year 10	$447,929	$516,137	$595,154	$686,560	$792,137	$913,894
14	Year 11	$491,805	$574,428	$671,869	$785,947	$920,036	$1,077,117
15	Year 12	$538,314	$637,382	$755,836	$897,260	$1,065,841	$1,266,456
16	Year 13	$587,612	$705,373	$848,420	$1,021,931	$1,232,059	$1,486,089
17	Year 14	$639,869	$778,803	$950,262	$1,161,563	$1,421,547	$1,740,884
18	Year 15	$695,261	$858,107	$1,062,288	$1,317,951	$1,637,563	$2,036,402
19	Year 16	$753,977	$943,756	$1,185,517	$1,493,105	$1,883,822	$2,379,226
20	Year 17	$816,216	$1,036,256	$1,321,069	$1,689,278	$2,164,557	$2,776,902
21							
22	Calculation = Previous Year Balance X the Percentage + the Previous Year Balance, + $17,000 Annual SEP Contribution.						
23	Example - $125,000 X 0.06 (6%) = $7,500 + $125,000 + $17,000 = $149,500						

It looks like Howard will have to return an average of 8% ROI over the next seventeen years to accumulate a million dollars. Don't forget he has done the most conservative calculations, and he is also going to make the deposits to the savings account which is different from this SEP account. The savings accumulated can also be held in certificates of deposits, or he could open up non-retirement on-line stock trading account. Of course, it would be taxed, but it still provides the potential for a good ROI.

Next, Howard and his wife need to get specific on how they will move toward their life endeavors. There are so many ways they can make changes to get where they want to go. The kids are essentially done with high school; so, there is no reason they may not want to factor downsizing their house and moving to another area where they can yet save even more money. Perhaps Howard's wife wants to pursue working again, now that the kids are basically grown. No one likes change, but when we have a specific plan and direction to our lives changing is much easier. It is all part of our journey towards our endeavors.

Howard will then list all his tasks and events, place them in chronological order and then create a timeline. He will make reviews of how it is going, and he is on his way.

We won't go into detail on this because we already did it for Sam Single. Refer to Sam's scenario for specifics.

Chapter 15 – Tracy's Implementation

Planning – Step 1 (Implementation)

If you recall, Tracy is in a controlled environment. Her husband does not allow her to leave the house on her own. She has to be accompanied by either him or one of the daughters. He keeps her cleaning the house, and mostly remedial jobs. He handles all the money and budgeting, and gives her money like an allowance, but only after she is required to justify it. He requires her to go with him when he travels to buy new business equipment, and generally does not impart any trust. The fact is, she is a strong willed person, and an intelligent person, but after years of such abuse she succumbs to his demands to keep peace in order that her daughters can finish through high school without another divorce. It has affected her self-esteem, and has her in a state of depression routinely.

She has been waiting until the girls are through high school, and then she will leave her husband. The youngest daughter (not her biological daughter but her husband's physically impaired daughter, Carina) is now fifteen years old, and so what Tracy has dreamed of is only a few years off. She has determined that she wants to pursue a business in interior and exterior design. She now needs to create an implementation plan for all this to happen. Her plan is simple compared to many, but will involve some very emotional issues. Here's what she anticipates:

1. She will attempt to start saving money right now to assist her departure. She will need money to bridge the time between separating from her husband and starting a new job. Money will also help when it comes to legal assistance during a divorce.

2. Next, she will live with one of her sisters when she initially separates. This will save her money, and provide emotional support during this time.

3. Next, she will get a job to support herself, probably a factory job since that is where her work experience lies. If she can get a job at a landscaping or interior design company that would be a plus, but it would have to supply an adequate wage.

4. Next, she will save money towards starting her own business.

5. As she is saving money and working at her new job she will start thinking about the specifics of how to start her business. She will read some books, and do an implementation plan with timeline and business plan.

6. Tracy has decided that a four-year degree is not necessarily needed for the kind of business she wants to operate. She has been on the internet and has found several trade school type courses that would provide both information on interior/exterior design, as well as general business operation.

7. She understands that money may be better spent on some counseling during the emotional readjustment time immediately after the

separation. She wants to succeed, but knows she needs to at least get some fulfillment in the area of safety, love and esteem.

There are some other "unknowns" and "factors" that may become a part of her plan. For example, she receives a significant disability payment from a company she worked for from an accident she incurred resulting in leg therapy. She is able to work now, but the payments are on-going. Also, she receives child support for her two daughters from a previous marriage. Currently, both of these entitlements are turned over directly to her husband who uses them at his discretion; usually for his business purposes. Some of these payments may be able to assist her later.

Tracy definitely has several "phases" to her plan. Phases are needed because it is hard to plan succeeding phases that are usually related to the success or outcome of the previous phase. For this reason, Phase I would typically be defined in detail while Phase II, III, etc. would be defined in very general terms. At the end of each Phase, then the next Phase would be defined and implemented in detail.

For Tracy Phase I consists of saving money, researching a little about interior and exterior design (internet), and arranging for assistance from her brother, sisters and family. Concerning the saving of money, it will be difficult to save money since she has little exposure to it. She may have to use some underhanded methods to achieve what she needs to do. In her mind, she has no problem justifying saving money equal to what she gets from child support and disability; since that is supposed to be her money anyway. She even feels some money due from when she has worked at the factory. It is going to be tough for Tracy to save money in most of the ways listed in this book or the ways some of the other example people have used because she has to do it in secrecy from her husband, and she has almost no access to any of their money. She does, however, have the support and understanding of her brother, sisters and teenage daughters. Don't forget that two of her daughters came with her to this marriage, and her current husband is their stepfather. They have not liked the way he has treated their mother. Here's what she came up with as ways to save some money:

1. **Savings Storage** – First and foremost, Tracy has a problem with storing whatever money she may be able to save. She can't open up or use an existing bank savings account because her husband would more than likely find out about it (e.g. by mailed account statements, annual interest statements, etc.). Another problem is that Tracy has little access to the bank, unless she can do it while she is grocery shopping with one of her daughters. She is almost forced to hide cash temporarily somewhere in the house. She can do that, but she would eventually want to put it in a safer place when the amount becomes significant. She talked to one of her sisters about this problem and they worked out another option. Tracy would save money at home until it reached $500 or more and then she would buy a money order and send it to her sister out of state. Her sister would then put it into a savings account under her own name.

2. **Daughter's Assistance** – Tracy is very close to her daughters. The two teenage daughters that came to this marriage with her share everything. They were quite aware of Tracy's situation, and Tracy shared all her dreams with them. When

Tracy told them of her plan and endeavor they both wanted to help. They went through the list of ideas on saving money in this book. As teenage daughters they did need money all the time to go to events, hang with their friends, buy clothes, etc. One of the daughters had a job and a car. She calculated that she could give Tracy about 1/3 of what she earned to go into the savings plan. Both daughters said they would cut back on their needs for clothes and entertainment and allow Tracy to pocket what is saved.

3. **Cash Instead of Credit Card** – Tracy used both cash and the credit card, but knew if she started using cash more that she could save some by not spending all of it. In other words, if she had $200 to spend on groceries and only needed $160 she could keep the difference.

4. **Miscellaneous Purchases** – When Tracy and her daughters put their minds to it they came up with a lot of items they could budget better for. There are so many things that women use that a man just takes for granted are needed or doesn't understand. For example, they spend money on women's magazines, self-help books (like this one), cosmetics, hair styling products, etc. Other things like car gasoline, soft drinks, candy, gum, snacks, etc. were places where money could be saved by just cutting back on these items. Tracy and the girls decided many of these things they could do without.

5. **Loose Change** – Saving loose change was definitely a good idea because Tracy and the

girls did all the clothes washing, and cleaning. Tracy retrieved lots of change from pocket cleaning before laundering, loose change placed on the coffee table and nightstand, etc. She had always saved it, but ended up using it when she was short on cash. Now she could save it.

6. **Garage Sale** – A garage sale was another excellent idea for Tracy. Her girls could assist, and she knew her husband would not want to be involved. The girls had tons of things they want to get rid of, and thought it was a great way to save money for Tracy.

Now, some of the above ideas are devious in nature, and I am not one to believe cheating or deceiving is a very good idea. Not only is it against good values, but if it helps one get to where they are going then they might start to think it's ok. It's not ok, and honesty and integrity are two of the most important human characteristics. However, I do believe that some people are placed into situations that require extreme measures to save mental and emotional health. In Tracy's case, money that she contributed to the marriage (like factory income, previous marriage alimony, child support, and disability income) always went to her husband, and she had no say in the budgeting process.

If you are a Tracy, or you know someone that is a Tracy, then you must always remember that your integrity is crucial to your life. It is so difficult to make decisions in life that may adversely affect yourself or others. A Tracy should always seek to do things in an honest and forthright way, but unfortunately life is full of situations that can't always be resolved in such a manner. None of us are ever "above the law," and we should always recognize this; however, "self-defense" is a defendable action. Self-defense to our mental health and well-being may require drastic measures. No one should be routinely abused at anytime – especially not in a free country.

It would be easy for me to just use average or "normal" scenario situations, but we can't ignore the fact that living conditions are very diverse, even in the USA. I have included these three scenario people because I wanted to include a variety of ways to think about ourselves and how to get where we need to go. Sometimes we remain stagnant because we only think in terms of our own sheltered lives. Perhaps by including Tracy's situation it will help us to recognize that we must always try and include all options or alternatives available. Of course as I have already stated (and will do so again):

We must always remain honest and uphold our integrity. Getting somewhere dishonestly may provide some relief, but can we live with ourselves after that? We lose trust in ourselves, and others lose trust in us also. What good is life without trust?

This concludes Ron's soapbox speech on morality (lighten up, Ron).

Chapter 16 - Life, Liberty and Happiness

So what have I been babbling on about throughout this book? Let's review and summarize. "Happiness" seems to be something pretty important in life. In fact, I'd have to say it is maybe the most important thing in life. We live on this earth for only a short time, and we want to be happy. If you live in the USA, then you among 5% of the world population that already has the two requirements to allow you to pursue happiness. That is, you are alive (life), and you are free (liberty). There are so many other people in the world that don't have one or both of these requirements, and never will. So, you have the best chance of obtaining happiness.

We are constantly looking for things to make us happy – like material possessions, love from others, power and control of our surroundings, etc., but I believe there may be some main endeavor that each of us can pursue that will make us happier than jumping from one thing to another. I'm not saying we can't be interested in more than one thing, and that we can't enjoy material items in life. I'm saying that we should make an effort to determine what endeavor makes us happiest, and spend our valuable time pursuing it. Regardless of whether we are pursuing our true life endeavor or not, we do need to have an endeavor and a plan of action, or else we get bogged down worrying about inconsequential things called mind clutter.

In initially determining your life endeavor you must eliminate all perceived obstacles. In other words, you must assume you have all the resources to pursue your self-actualization, and all obligations to others have been met. Never worry about the "how" because there is always a way to make things happen when we are "focused" and "determined." So many of us are good at seeing and worrying about barriers to success – we need to change our outlook or view of life. Barriers are simply obstacles that can be overcome when we feel that we know what we want to do.

This pursuance of our endeavor gives us control over our lives, and that is very important. Most people probably don't feel they have control over their daily lives or their future. The reason is because they are trying to focus on the wrong things. By "trying" I mean that there are so many activities and thoughts in the mind that one cannot focus on all of them, and then they begin to clutter the mind. People are busy trying to please others, or acting out of guilt or just not sure what to do. A direction in life eliminates mind clutter.

Ok, so foremost in life we need to have direction and a plan. This will allow us to have control of our life. Much of the rest of this book has to do with how to help us stay on course with this pursuance of our endeavor. By recognizing more about ourselves (self-introspection) and more about others (human behavior) we will less likely be slowed down trying to deal with human interaction we don't understand. We will be able to determine what is important and what isn't. We will develop a "big picture" mindset.

So much of what we accomplish is a function of our expectations. We derive our expectations from our experiences in life and by the way we are raised. Understanding some about human nature, as well as about ourselves will help us to adjust our expectations, as well as to be comfortable with changing them when needed.

Also, knowing more about human behavior such as motivational needs (Maslow) will help us to understand why we act the way we do. We can now know that safety, love, esteem, etc. are needs not to be confused with life endeavors. As Maslow stated, "needs" go away once they are satisfied. A life endeavor (self-actualization) goes on forever. See, knowing a little about needs will help us to make sure we are defining "endeavors" and not "needs."

In addition, we need to motivate ourselves constantly to make sure we stay on course. It is so easy to feel sorry for ourselves, but we must constantly strive for a positive attitude, and constantly remind ourselves of how lucky we are. Remember that even though we have defined our endeavor and created a plan, that life is continually about choices, sacrifices, concessions and compromises. Therefore, we must make an effort to motivate ourselves in order to keep our endeavor in focus – "Out of sight, out of mind." We can do this by many methods:

- Find some person or persons in your life that have succeeded in the face of adversity, and think about how you admire their ability to cope with life on a daily basis.

- Read biographies of inspirational people (e.g. Abraham Lincoln, Teddy Roosevelt, J.C. Penney, etc.).

- Select movies that make you happy and inspire you to be more than you are (Seabiscuit, Hoosiers, The Natural, etc.)

- Find inspirational quotes and clichés that remind you to think positively, and live a life of

169

happiness. Pin these quotes up where you can see them.

- Inspire yourself by looking around and noticing the lives of others, and compare how lucky you are.

- Do some routine volunteer work at a hospital, hospice or retirement home.

- Every morning, just as routine as brushing your teeth, read a motivational note that you have written to yourself. If it becomes ineffective after a while write a new one. See the following example:

"I am fortunate to have the freedoms and opportunities I have living in this country. Even when things seem bad they are no way near as bad as the conditions that the majority of people in the world experience as a normal day. People have given their lives in battle so that I may enjoy these freedoms and opportunities. So many people have come to this country with so much less than I have, and have achieved so much more because they appreciate these opportunities, and don't take them for granted. They are happy to be here. Many of my neighbors are burdened by health and medical problems. Some have children and other loved ones with permanent physical disabilities or terminal illnesses. These people bear these burdens, many times with a smile on their face and hope in their hearts. Therefore, I am going to live my life to the fullest, and demonstrate my gratitude to those that died in battle and those less fortunate that have succeeded. So today I will smile, and be cheerful so others will follow my way. I will "Do unto others as I would have others do unto me." "Integrity" and "Determination"

will be my guides. I am alive for one more day, and I am thankful!"

Another way to motivate yourself is to maintain your own health and body. Exercise, get in shape and feel good about yourself. This "feeling good about yourself" does not mean you have to be in perfect shape, but rather in control of your health. If you are diabetic, for instance, and you are exercising, taking medication, and are able to keep your blood sugar level within range routinely – then you will feel good about yourself. It is a relative thing, defined by your "standards." You are in control.

Once you have an endeavor to pursue you must have a plan to implement it. Following the ISO format to implementing such ongoing programs is an excellent way to do this. First, determine what resources you will need. Then list everything and assign a projected cost and length of time it will take to complete each task. Next, arrange the tasks in order or chronology, and make a time chart. Charts and review sessions will help to monitor and measure your progress. Remember, we must always be reviewing and analyzing where we are going and how we are doing. If we don't then the process will fail because:

Out of Sight, Out of Mind

Chapter 17 - In Closing

There are some things in life that many people take for granted, but when we actually take a good look around, we find out they aren't as we expect. Many of these things seem trivial in the realm of life, but actually make a difference in how we, as humans, get along in life. I'm talking about human behavior, communications, impressions and expectations. Many "rules of thumb," "sayings" and "clichés" related to these things have been passed down through the generations. I have listed some points that I believe are important for each of us to consider in making our way through this world.

- Be courteous, kind and polite.

- Be who you are and not what you think others think you are.

- Forget the Joneses.

- Find someone to love, and share your life.

- We need to "live this life" – it's all we have.

- People are important. Life is about people, so we need to learn how to better understand them and ourselves so we can communicate and live better with each other.

- Related to the above we all need to be more aware of our surroundings and how we are affecting others, and how they are affecting us.

We need to be aware of self-centeredness, self-indulgence, and human behavior, and appreciate what we have, etc.

- Integrity is so important. It makes us feel good about ourselves, and it is what builds credibility with others.

- Be a leader and not a follower when it comes to control of your life – it is your life and you know where you want to go. If you fail or succeed make it because you made the decisions, not because you followed someone else.

- Apologize whenever you are wrong. And don't just give a weak apology – give a meaningful apology and use the word "apologize." Don't you remember that people appreciate it when you admit to being wrong because then you are human like them? Nobody knows everything. It makes us feel good afterward, and it makes them feel good also. It's almost like a compliment. For us to admit wrong doing is difficult and demonstrates that we put people and their feelings and integrity above our own pride and bull-headedness. How many times have you seen where a celebrity or popular well-know figure denies the truth? In the end it almost always turns out that if they had just been honest and forthright with people then they would have been a lot better off. People are forgiving and understanding to those that admit and truly are sorry for their wrong-doings. Everyone sins. It is much easier for us to forget and forgive when the person "owns up" to their actions (takes responsibility). It is hard to ever believe or put credibility in people that seem to go out of their way to lie and deceive. Don't do it!

- Remember, as hard as we may try we are limited by our genetic makeup. Some things will come easier for us while other things will be harder. Some people are born with more drive and determination, but we can be happy if we know that we have some control and understanding of our bodies, mind and physical qualities.

- Finally, "Never Give Up." Remember that with desire, fortitude and determination we humans can do anything. You can control your health, your daily life and your destiny.

Bibliography

1. Brown, H. Jackson, Jr., <u>Life's Little Instruction Book</u>, Rutledge Hill Press, Nashville TN, 1991.

2. Fujita, Frank, Nurture vs Nature… Yada, yada

3. Green, Christopher D., *Classics in the History of Psychology (A.H. Maslow (1943) A Theory of Human Motivation*, Psychology Review, 50, pp. 370-396.

4. Boeree, George C. (Dr.), *Abraham Maslow 1908-1970*, Personality Theories, 1998.

5. Bremer, Jill, <u>The Power of First Impressions</u>, Bremer Communications, 2004.

6. Norwood, George, *Maslow's Hierarchy of Needs*, 1996.

7. Davis, *Abraham Maslow, Understanding Human Motivation*, University of Toledo, 2004.

8. B.B. Skinner Foundation, Brief *Biography of B.F. Skinner*, 2004.

9. Hammonds, K., Cole, A., and Hartill, E., *Skinner's Defense of Behaviorism, Classic Works, Animal Learning Theory and Utopian Societies*, Wabash College, 2003.

10. Stevensen, David, *Sigmund Freud: The Father of Psychoanalysis*, Brown University, 2003.

11. Wikholm, Andrew, *Biography: Alfred Kinsey*, 1999.

12. Hite, Shere, <u>The Shere Hite Reader</u>, 1999.

13. Severo, Richard, *William H. Masters, a Pioneer in Studying and Demystifying Sex, Dies at 85*, New York Times, 2001.

14. Trochim, W.M.K., *Statistical Sampling Terms*, Research Methods Knowledge Base, 2001.

15. Murray, Charles, *"The Bell Curve" and its Critics*, Upstream, 1995.

16. The Wall Street Journal, *Mainstream Science on Intelligence*, Upstream, 1994.

17. *Analyzing the Bell Curve*, Ben's Bell Curve page, 2003.

18. Case, James, Is *the Bell Curve Statistically Sound?*, SIA News, Vol-28, No.-1, 1995.

19. National Vital Statistics Reports, Vol. 52, No. 9, November 7, 2003, Table E, Population Reference Bureau, www.prb.org.

About the Author

Ron Himebaugh is 57 years old, and was born to a middle class, blue-collar family with one older brother and one younger sister. Music was a big part of his family environment. His father played the trombone in big bands, as well as the guitar, bass and piano. He still plays piano in the dining room of an upscale retirement facility, as well as in a weekly jazz group. Ron's mother played piano, and his brother is an accomplished classical and jazz pianist. His sister played the flute in high school, and now also plays the guitar and bass. Ron played the trombone in the high school band and orchestra. He now plays classical style guitar, and occasionally plays at area restaurants and events. Ron is also a member of SPEBSQSA (The Society for the Preservation and Encouragement of Barber Shop Quartet Singing in America). He is part of the chorus as well as occasional quartets.

Ron's father was a true trouble-shooter and problem solver when he worked at NCR. He was an electrician that peaked during the age of early computer evolution. Ron's brother and sister, both have Masters Degrees in Mathematics and Accounting, respectively. Ron has a Masters in Chemistry and a B.S. in Biology/Botany.

Ron's career path began in the analytical water and wastewater laboratory of Montgomery County, Ohio. He eventually became Superintendent of Wastewater Systems over two different counties. During that time he obtained his Masters Degree in Chemistry, and taught evening courses in treatment and laboratory procedures for the Ohio Environmental Protection Agency (EPA) Operator Training Committee. As part of his Masters thesis, Ron developed a new method for the determination of Chemical Oxygen

Demand in water. The method became recognized and placed as a world standard in: *The Standard Methods for the Examination of Water and Wastewater*.

Ron left his local government position to become Midwest Representative of Polybac Corporation; a cutting edge company involved in the treatment and ultimate disposal of hazardous wastes and chemicals by use of microbiological organisms (selectively, adapted mutant bacteria). These applications included the cleanup of oil spills, ocean spills, and industrial chemical wastewaters.

Ron wrote several magazine articles and co-authored a textbook used throughout the world in the operation of wastewater treatment facilities. He also gave numerous technical papers and served as an instructor at the Center for Professional Advancement in New Jersey.

Ron started his own business in 1983 when the use of personal computers emerged. He designed software applications first for reporting monthly data to State Environmental Regulatory Agencies, and then applications for Preventive/Corrective Maintenance and Human Resources management. His services eventually expanded into Environmental, Health and Safety (EHS) consulting, as well as, management training. During those years Ron became certified by NASHP as a Professional Hazards Manager (PHM) and an Occupational Safety Professional (OSP). He became a Registered Environmental Professional (REP) through NREP, and was named as a member in "Who's Who in Environmental, Health and Safety Training by NETA. In 1996 an international standard to environmental management was introduced and Ron became a certified auditor for this ISO 14000 standard.

The majority of Ron's career has dealt with problem solving and management of people and situations. He has had courses in supervisory management provided by Michigan University, and has been a member of the American Management Association. In college Ron took several psychology courses including Logic, Ethics and Advertising Psychology. Ron was confirmed in the Lutheran church, and took courses in New Testament Thought as an undergraduate student in college.

Although considered successful and fortunate by both himself and others, Ron has endured war, business failure and personal health problems. After graduation from college in 1969 he was drafted into the Army and served a 13-month tour in Vietnam as a machine gunner and infantryman. While in the jungles of the South Vietnam Central Highlands Ron was "field" promoted four positions in one day to Buck Sergeant to command a squad. After five months he was moved into base camp to become the company clerk and administrator because he had a college degree and could type. Shortly thereafter, most of his company was killed in a mortar attack at a firebase, and his machine gun squad was killed when they walked into an ambush. Ron says, "His college degree saved his life."

Ron's business was reduced to failure when a local bank reneged on a promised loan. The bank had been bought out, and the original Loan Officer had been indicted for a credit card scam through the bank. The Loan Officer that replaced him was then removed for embezzling money from the bank. Although the business was progressing as anticipated it could not endure the lengthy negotiations and requirements made by the bank. He lost everything in bankruptcy. Later, Ron learned that two other companies had been placed into the same situation and they had successfully sued the bank. As a young business owner he was unaware that he had such legal recourse. With the assistance of valued business relationships Ron had made throughout his career he was able to rebuild the business and make it even more successful.

Ron developed Type II Diabetes in 1996. Doing much of his own research into the disease he worked closely with his family doctor and endocrinologist to control the disease effectively. In the summer of 2002 he was required to have a pacemaker. Recently, 2002, research and data analysis by the government determined that both Ron's diabetes and heart problem most likely are due to exposure to Agent Orange, a chemical defoliant used in Vietnam.

With Gun and Holster

College

Vietnam 1970

Mid 70's

**Graduate's method
becomes world standard**

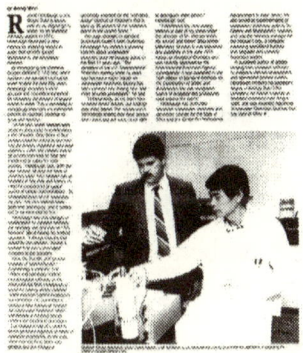

Std Method Development
in 70's

Early 80's

Early 90's

2002

Favorite Pastime

Barbershop Quartet
"Singing Valentine"